CONTENTS

3

BREAKFAST RECIPES

Grilled Asian-style Broccoli

Servings: 4 Slices
Cooking Time: 10 Minutes
Ingredients:
- 4 tablespoons soy sauce
- 4 tablespoons balsamic vinegar
- 2 tablespoons canola oil
- 2 teaspoons maple syrup
- 2 heads broccoli, trimmed into florets
- Red pepper flakes, for garnish
- Sesame seeds, for garnish

Directions:
1. Preheat the griddle to medium high.
2. While the unit is preheating, in a large bowl, whisk together the soy sauce, balsamic vinegar, oil, and maple syrup. Add the broccoli and toss to coat evenly.
3. Place the broccoli on the Grill and grill for 8 to 10 minutes, until charred on all sides.
4. When cooking is complete, place the broccoli on a large serving platter. Garnish with red pepper flakes and sesame seeds. Serve immediately.

Nutrition Info: (Per serving): Calories: 133kcal; Fat: 8g; Carbs: 13g; Protein: 5g

Light And Fluffy Buttermilk Pancakes

Servings: 2
Cooking Time: 10 Minutes
Ingredients:
- 2 cups all-purpose flour
- 3 tablespoons sugar
- 2 teaspoons baking powder
- 2 teaspoons baking soda
- pinch kosher salt
- 2 eggs
- 2½ cups buttermilk

Directions:
1. Preparing the Ingredients.
2. Sift the flour, sugar, baking powder, baking soda, and salt together in a large bowl.
3. In a medium bowl, Beat the eggs, buttermilk, and melted butter together until frothy, then pour into the dry ingredients. Mix until well combined but do not overmix. Small lumps will be fine. Let sit at room temperature for 20 to 30 Minutes while your grill heats up.
4. Bring the griddle grill to medium-high heat. Oil the griddle and allow it to heat until the oil is shimmering but not smoking.
5. Grilling
6. Pour about ¼ cup batter onto the griddle grill for each pancake. The pancakes should slowly begin to form bubbles. After 2 to 4 Minutes, when the bubbles pop and leave small holes, flip the pancake. Cook for an additional 2 Minutes.

Hash Brown Scramble

Servings: 4
Cooking Time: 10 Minutes
Ingredients:
- 2 russet potatoes, shredded, rinsed, and drained
- 8 eggs, beaten
- 1 cup cheddar cheese
- 6 slices bacon, cut into small pieces
- 1/3 cup green onion, chopped
- vegetable oil

Directions:
1. Preheat griddle to medium heat and brush with vegetable oil.
2. On one side, place the potatoes on the griddle and spread in a 1/2 inch thick layer. Cook the potatoes until golden brown and then flip. Add the bacon to the other side of the griddle and cook until the fat has rendered.
3. Add the eggs and cheese to the top of the hash browns and stir in the bacon and green onion. Cook until the cheese has melted and divide equally among 4 plates.

Nutrition Info: Calories: 470, Sodium: 965 mg, Dietary Fiber: 2.8g, Fat:30.2g,Carbs: 18.8g Protein: 30.6g

Figs With Honey

Servings: 4
Cooking Time: 25 Minutes
Ingredients:

- 8 ripe figs, stemmed
- 2 tablespoons walnut oil or good-quality olive oil
- 8 walnut halves, toasted
- ¼ cup honey

Directions:
1. Preparing the Ingredients.
2. Brush the figs with the walnut oil, then cut an X in the stem ends. Push 1 walnut half into each fig.
3. Grilling
4. Heat your Griddle to medium heat.
5. Place the figs on the grill, stem side up. Cook until the fruit softens, 5 to 10 Minutes. Transfer to a platter, spry with the honey, and serve.

Grilling Repes

Servings: 8
Cooking Time: 15 Minutes
Ingredients:
- 1 cup all-purpose flour
- 1½ cups milk
- ½ cup water
- 2 eggs
- 1 teaspoon grated lemon zest
- 2 pinches salt
- 2 tablespoons melted butter, plus more as needed for the griddle

Directions:
1. Preparing the Ingredients.
2. Place all the ingredients except the butter in a blender and Mixfor 30 to 45 seconds until a smooth batter forms. If necessary, scrape down the sides of the blender so all the ingredients are incorporated, and Mixagain. Allow the batter to rest for 30 Minutes.
3. Bring the griddle grill to medium heat. Butter about a 10-inch square on the griddle grill, then pour ¼ cup of the batter in the center.
4. Grilling
5. Spread the crepe batter into a circle with the measuring cup or use a crepe spreader to create a thin, round layer on the griddle. Cook for about 90 seconds or until most of the batter has set. Flip and cook for another 60 to 90 seconds until it is between yellow and golden brown in color. (You can cook the crepes to your desired doneness, but I find Grilling

them to a yellowish color leaning toward golden brown is best for rolling and stuffing.)

Chocolate Lava Cake

Servings: 8
Cooking Time: 30 Minutes
Ingredients:
- ½ pound (2 sticks) butter, plus softened butter for the pan
- 8 ounces dark chocolate, chopped
- 4 eggs
- 4 egg yolks
- ½ cup sugar
- 4 teaspoons all-purpose flour
- ½ teaspoon salt

Directions:
1. Preparing the Ingredients.
2. Generously coat the inside of a 9- or 10-inch cast-iron skillet with softened butter; make sure not to miss any spots, or the cake will stick.
3. Place the ½ pound butter in a heatproof bowl and melt it in the microwave or over hot water in a double boiler. Add the chocolate to the hot butter and mix until it's melted.
4. Place the whole eggs and egg yolks in another bowl. Add the sugar and Whisk with an electric mixer on high speed (or enthusiastically with a whisk) until light and thick, about 1 minute. On low speed (or whisking) Whisk the egg mixture, flour, and salt into the melted chocolate and butter until combined. Pour the batter into the prepared pan. (At this point you can refrigerate the batter for up to 3 hours; take the pan out of the refrigerator 30 Minutes before you intend to bake it.)
5. If using a Griddle, heat for medium direct
6. Grilling
7. The grill temperature should be 500° to 600°F; it could mean all the burners are on medium or medium-low, depending on your particular grill.
8. Place the pan on the grill directly. Grill-bake until the cake puffs up around the edge but the center still jiggles slightly when shaken, 5 to 15 Minutes. (It's better to underbake than to overbake the cake; start checking it after 3 Minutes.) Let sit for at least

10 Minutes before slicing, or the insides will ooze all over the pan.

Pumpkin Pancake

Servings: 4
Cooking Time: 10 Minutes
Ingredients:
- 4 eggs
- 1/2 tsp cinnamon
- 1/2 cup pumpkin puree
- 1 cup almond flour
- 2 tsp liquid stevia
- 1 tsp baking powder

Directions:
1. Preheat the griddle to medium-low heat.
2. In a bowl, mix almond flour, stevia, baking powder, cinnamon, pumpkin puree, and eggs until well combined.
3. Spray griddle top with cooking spray.
4. Drop batter onto the hot griddle top.
5. Cook pancakes until lightly golden brown from both sides.
6. Serve and enjoy.
Nutrition Info: (Per Serving): Calories 235 ;Fat 18.5 g ;Carbohydrates 9.6 g ;Sugar 2.4 g ;Protein 11.9 g ;Cholesterol 164 mg

Ultimate Breakfast Burrito

Servings: 2
Cooking Time: 20 Minutes
Ingredients:
- 4 eggs
- 4 strips bacon
- 1 large russet potato, peeled and cut into small cubes
- 1 red bell pepper
- 1/2 yellow onion
- 1 ripe avocado, sliced
- 2 tablespoon hot sauce
- 2 large flour tortillas
- vegetable oil

Directions:
1. Preheat the griddle to medium-high heat on one side and medium heat on the other side. Brush with vegetable oil and add the bacon to the medium heat side and peppers and onions to the medium-high side.
2. When the bacon finishes cooking, place on paper towels and chop into small pieces. Add the potatoes to the bacon fat on the griddle. Cook the potatoes until softened.
3. Add the eggs to the vegetable side and cook until firm. Place the ingredients onto the tortillas and top with slices of avocado and a tablespoon of hot sauce. Fold the tortillas and enjoy.
Nutrition Info: Calories: 793, Sodium: 1800 mg, Dietary Fiber: 10.7g, Fat: 41.3.g, Carbs: 73.4g Protein: 35.8g

Jalapeño Stuffed Burger

Servings: 4
Cooking Time: 50 Minutes
Ingredients:
- Burger Mixture
- 2 lb. ground beef
- 1 tsp. sea salt
- 1 tsp. ground black pepper
- 3 tbsp. cilantro, chopped ½ small onion, peeled & minced
- 1 jalapeño, seeded & chopped

Directions:
1. Preparing the Ingredients.
2. Combine ground beef, sea salt, pepper, cilantro, onion, and jalapeño. Divide ground beef mixture into 4 balls. Stuff each ball with a chunk of cheddar. Rub burgers with olive oil. Grill
3. Grilling
4. About 5 Minutes per side or to desired doneness. Top burgers with sliced cheddar.
5. Spread each roll with margarine. Grill to desired doneness. Serve burgers topped with pickled jalapeños. 4 ½ oz. cheddar cheese, cut into chunks 2 tbsp. olive oil,4 slices cheddar cheese,4 brioche rolls ¼ cup margarine,16 pickled jalapeño rings. If you have fresh sliced jalapeños, heat 1 cup vinegar and ¼ cup sugar, then pour over the peppers and let sit for 30 Minutes for a quick pickle.

Spinach Pancakes

Servings: 6
Cooking Time: 10 Minutes
Ingredients:

- 4 eggs
- 1 cup coconut milk
- 1/4 cup chia seeds
- 1 cup spinach, chopped
- 1/2 tsp black pepper
- 1/2 tsp ground nutmeg
- 1 tsp baking soda
- 1/2 cup coconut flour
- 1/2 tsp salt

Directions:

1. In a bowl, whisk eggs with coconut milk until frothy.
2. Mix together all dry ingredients and add in the egg mixture and whisk until smooth.
3. Add spinach and stir well.
4. Preheat the griddle to medium-low heat.
5. Spray griddle top with cooking spray.
6. Pour 3-4 tablespoons of batter onto the hot griddle top and make a round pancake.
7. Cook pancake until lightly golden brown from both sides.
8. Serve and enjoy.

Nutrition Info: (Per Serving): Calories 111 ;Fat 7 g ;Carbohydrates 5 g ;Sugar 0.4 g ;Protein 6.3 g ;Cholesterol 109 mg

Classic Denver Omelet

Servings: 2
Cooking Time: 10 Minutes
Ingredients:

- 6 large eggs
- 1/4 cup country ham, diced
- 1/4 cup yellow onion, finely chopped
- 1/4 cup green bell pepper, chopped
- 2/3 cup cheddar cheese, shredded
- 1/4 teaspoon cayenne pepper
- salt and black pepper
- 2 tablespoons butter

Directions:

1. Heat your griddle to medium heat and place the butter onto the griddle.
2. Add the ham, onion, and pepper to the butter and cook until the vegetables have just softened.
3. Beat the eggs in a large bowl and add a pinch of salt and the cayenne pepper.
4. Split the vegetables into to portions on the griddle and add half of the eggs to each portion. Cook until the eggs have begun to firm up, and then add the cheese to each omelet.
5. Fold the omelets over and remove from the griddle. Serve immediately.

Nutrition Info: Calories: 507, Sodium: 747 mg, Dietary Fiber: 0.8g, Fat: 40.5g, Carbs: 4.9g Protein: 31.5g

Baked Egg And Bacon–stuffed Peppers

Servings: 4
Cooking Time: 15 Minutes
Ingredients:

- 1 cup shredded Cheddar cheese
- 4 slices bacon, cooked and chopped
- 4 bell peppers, seeded and tops removed
- 4 large eggs
- Sea salt
- Freshly ground black pepper
- Chopped fresh parsley, for garnish

Directions:

1. Preheat the griddle to medium high.
2. Divide the cheese and bacon between the bell peppers. Crack one of the eggs into each bell pepper, and season with salt and pepper.
3. Place each bell pepper to the grill and cook for 10 to 15 minutes, until the egg whites are cooked and the yolks are slightly runny.
4. Remove the peppers, garnish with parsley, and serve.

Nutrition Info: (Per serving): Calories: 326kcal; Fat: 23g; Carbs: 10g; Protein: 22g

Grilled Pizza With Eggs And Greens

Servings: 2 Slices
Cooking Time: 8 Minutes
Ingredients:

- 2 tbsps. all-purpose flour, plus more as needed
- 1/2 store-bought pizza dough (about 8 ounces)

- 1 tbsp. canola oil, divided
- 1 cup fresh ricotta cheese
- 4 large eggs
- Sea salt
- Freshly ground black pepper
- 4 cups arugula, torn
- 1 tbsp. extra-virgin olive oil
- 1 tsp. freshly squeezed lemon juice
- 2 tbsps. grated Parmesan cheese

Directions:

1. Preheat the griddle to medium high.
2. Dust a clean work surface with flour. Place the dough on the floured surface, and roll it into a 9-inch round of even thickness. Dust your rolling pin and work surface with additional flour, as needed, to ensure the dough does not stick.
3. Brush the surface of the rolled-out dough evenly with 1/2 tablespoon of canola oil. Flip the dough over and brush with the remaining 1/2 tablespoon oil. Poke the dough with a fork 5 or 6 times across its surface to prevent air pockets from forming during cooking.
4. Place the dough to the grill and cook for 4 minutes.
5. After 4 minutes, flip the dough, then spoon teaspoons of ricotta cheese across the surface of the dough, leaving a 1-inch border around the edges.
6. Crack one egg into a ramekin or small bowl. This way you can easily remove any shell that may break into the egg and keep the yolk intact. Imagine the dough is split into four quadrants. Pour one egg into each. Repeat with the remaining 3 eggs. Season the pizza with salt and pepper.
7. Continue cooking for the remaining 3 to 4 minutes, until the egg whites are firm.
8. Meanwhile, in a medium bowl, toss together the arugula, oil, and lemon juice, and season with salt and pepper.
9. Transfer the pizza to a cutting board and let it cool. Top it with the arugula mixture, drizzle with olive oil, if desired, and sprinkle with Parmesan cheese. Cut into pieces and serve.

Nutrition Info: (Per serving): Calories: 788kcal; Fat: 46g; Carbs: 58g; Protein: 34g

Diner Cilantro-style Omelet

Servings: 1
Cooking Time: 10 Minutes
Ingredients:
- ½ cup diced red bell pepper
- ½ cup sliced mushrooms
- ½ teaspoon garlic salt
- 2 eggs plus 2 egg yolks
- ½ cup shredded cheddar-Jack cheese blend, or 2 slices cheese
- butter, as needed
- salt and pepper, to taste
- cilantro, to serve (optional)

Directions:

1. Preparing the Ingredients.
2. Bring the griddle grill to medium-low heat.
3. Butter a portion of your griddle grill and begin to slowly sauté the peppers and mushrooms. After about 3 Minutes, give the veggies a mix and sprinkle on the garlic salt, then cover.
4. Whisk the eggs in a medium bowl until quite frothy. With a large spatula, move the pepper and mushroom mixture to the side of the griddle. Melt plenty of butter over a large area on the griddle and very slowly pour the eggs onto the Grilling surface. The eggs will run a bit, and if you are able to use the side of the spatula to shape them into a circle or square, they will be easier to flip later on.
5. Grilling
6. Allow the eggs to cook slowly without much poking or prodding. After about 3 Minutes, you will see the eggs start to bubble as they cook. Some portions of the omelet will be firm, and some portions will be runny and raw. Distribute the peppers and mushrooms evenly across the omelet the same way you would top a pizza, in a thin layer. When about 80 percent of the egg has solidified, add the cheese in an even layer.
7. At this point, your omelet should have very little runny or visibly raw egg remaining. With a long spatula, scrape under the omelet with a quick wrist motion to make sure the egg is released from the griddle before you attempt to finish. To fold the omelet in half, slide the spatula under the omelet until the entire width of the spatula is covered, and

with a lift and twist, lift the spatula and twist your wrist so the omelet folds over and flops onto itself.

8.   Cook for about another minute and serve with salt and pepper to taste. Garnish with cilantro, if desired

Easy Pita Bread

Servings: 6

Cooking Time: 2 Hours

Ingredients:

- 3 cups all-purpose or bread flour, plus more as needed
- 2 teaspoons instant yeast
- 2 teaspoons salt
- ½ teaspoon sugar
- 3 tablespoons good-quality olive oil
- 1 cup warm water, plus more as needed
- Melted butter for brushing (optional)

Directions:

1.   Preparing the Ingredients.

2.   Beat the flour, yeast, salt, and sugar together in a large bowl. Add the oil and water and mix with a heavy spoon. Continue to add water 1 tablespoon at a time, until the dough forms a ball and is slightly sticky; in the unlikely event that the mixture gets too sticky, add flour 1 tablespoon at a time.

3.   Turn the dough onto a lightly floured work surface and knead for a minute to form a smooth, round ball. Place the dough in a bowl and cover with plastic wrap; let rise in a warm spot until it doubles in size, 1 to 2 hours. Or you can let the dough rise more slowly, in the refrigerator, for up to 8 hours.

4.   Divide the dough into 6 to 12 even-sized pieces; roll each into a ball. Place each ball on a lightly floured surface and cover with plastic wrap or a clean dish towel. Let rest until they puff slightly, about 20 Minutes.

5.   On a lightly floured surface, roll each ball out to about ⅛ inch thick. Cover and let rest while you prepare the grill.

6.   Heat a Griddle for medium-high heat.

7.   Grilling

8.   Make sure the grates are clean.

9.   Working in batches, Place the breads on the grill directly. Cook turning once, until they're slightly

colored and puffed, 4 to 8 Minutes per side. Don't walk away from the grill. To use the pitas folded over fillings, cook them only until soft and pliable. If you're going to cut the pita in wedges for a dip or spread, you can grill them longer; move and rotate them for even Grilling. Transfer to a platter, brush with melted butter if you like, and serve.

French Toast Sticks

Servings: 2

Cooking Time: 10 Minutes

Ingredients:

- 2 eggs
- 4 bread slices, cut each bread slice into 3 pieces vertically
- 2/3 cup milk
- 1/4 tsp ground cinnamon
- 1 tsp vanilla

Directions:

1.   Preheat the griddle to medium-low heat.

2.   In a bowl, whisk eggs with cinnamon, vanilla, and milk.

3.   Spray griddle top with cooking spray.

4.   Dip each bread piece into the egg mixture and coat well.

5.   Place coated bread pieces onto the hot griddle top and cook until golden brown from both sides.

6.   Serve and enjoy.

Nutrition Info: (Per Serving): Calories 166 ;Fat 7 g ;Carbohydrates 14 g ;Sugar 5 g ;Protein 10.4 g ;Cholesterol 193 mg

Fluffy Blueberry Pancakes

Servings: 2

Cooking Time: 10 Minutes

Ingredients:

- 1 cup flour
- 3/4 cup milk
- 2 tablespoons white vinegar
- 2 tablespoons sugar
- 1 teaspoon baking powder
- 1/2 teaspoon baking soda
- 1/2 teaspoon salt
- 1 egg

- 2 tablespoons butter, melted
- 1cup fresh blueberries
- butter for cooking

Directions:

1. In a bowl, combine the milk and vinegar. Set aside for two minutes.
2. In a large bowl, combine the flour, sugar, baking powder, baking soda, and salt. Stir in the milk, egg, blueberries, and melted butter. Mix until combined but not totally smooth.
3. Heat your griddle to medium heat and add a little butter. Pour the pancakes onto the griddle and cook until one side is golden brown. Flip the pancakes and cook until the other side is golden.
4. Remove the pancakes from the griddle and serve with warm maple syrup.

Nutrition Info: Calories: 499, Sodium: 356 mg, Dietary Fiber: 3.5g, Fat: 16.5.g, Carbs: 76.2g Protein: 12.9g

Caramelized Oranges

Servings: 4
Cooking Time: 25 Minutes
Ingredients:

- ¼ cup sugar
- ½ teaspoon five-spice powder (to make your own
- 2 large oranges
- ¼ cup chopped fresh mint

Directions:

1. Preparing the Ingredients.
2. Mix the sugar and five-spice powder together on a small plate. Cut a sliver off the top and bottom of each orange so that it will sit flat on the grates without rolling, then turn them on their sides and cut in half through the equator. Remove any seeds. Press the cut side of each half into the sugar. Let sit until the sugar is absorbed and/or you are ready to grill.
3. Grilling
4. Heat your Griddle to medium heat. Place the orange halves on the grill directly, sugared side up.
5. Until they are warm all the way through, 5 to 10 Minutes. (Be careful not to let them stay on too long, or their juice will evaporate.) Turn them over and cook just until the cut sides brown, 2 to 3 Minutes.

Transfer to individual serving plates, sprinkle with the mint, and serve with a knife and fork or with grapefruit spoons, if you have them.

Grilled Peaches With Ginger Ice Cream

Servings: 4
Cooking Time: 40 Minutes
Ingredients:

- 1 pint vanilla ice cream, softened just a bit
- ¼ cup chopped candied ginger
- 2 or 4 ripe peaches, depending on their size
- 4 tablespoons (½ stick) butter, melted
- ¼ cup Demerara sugar, or more as needed
- Fresh mint sprigs for garnish

Directions:

1. Preparing the Ingredients.
2. Place the ice cream and ginger in a bowl and mash together with a wooden spoon until the ginger is mixed throughout the ice cream. This can be done several days ahead; Place it back in the ice cream container and freeze at least a couple hours.
3. Grilling
4. Heat your Griddle to medium heat. When you're ready for dessert, cut the peaches in half through the stem end and remove the pits. Brush with the melted butter. Place the sugar on a plate and dredge the cut side of each peach in it.
5. Place the peaches on the grill directly, cut side up. Cook until they soften, 10 to 15 Minutes depending on their size and ripeness. Turn them cut side down and cook until the sugar caramelizes to a golden brown, 2 to 5 Minutes. Transfer to a platter. To serve, Place the warm peaches on plates or in dessert bowls, cut side up. Divide the ice cream between them, or pass the ice cream at the table. Garnish with the mint.

Chocolate Pancake

Servings: 4
Cooking Time: 10 Minutes
Ingredients:

- 2 eggs
- 1/2 tsp baking powder
- 2 tbsp erythritol

- 1 1/2 tbsp cocoa powder
- 1/4 cup ground flaxseed
- 2 tbsp water
- 1 tsp nutmeg
- 1 tsp cinnamon
- 1/4 tsp salt

Directions:

1. In a bowl, mix ground flaxseed, baking powder, erythritol, cocoa powder, spices, and salt.
2. Add eggs and stir well.
3. Add water and stir until batter is well combined.
4. Preheat the griddle to medium-low heat.
5. Spray griddle top with cooking spray.
6. Pour a large spoonful of batter on a hot griddle top and make a pancake.
7. Cook pancake for 3-4 minutes on each side.
8. Serve and enjoy.

Nutrition Info: (Per Serving): Calories 138 ;Fat 12 g ;Carbohydrates 11 g ;Sugar 8 g ;Protein 4.5 g ;Cholesterol 82 mg

Spicy Egg Scrambled

Servings: 2
Cooking Time: 10 Minutes
Ingredients:

- 4 eggs
- 2 tbsp cilantro, chopped
- 1/3 cup heavy cream
- 1 tomato, diced
- 3 tbsp butter
- 1 Serrano chili pepper, chopped
- 2 tbsp scallions, sliced
- 1/4 tsp pepper
- 1/2 tsp salt

Directions:

1. Preheat the griddle to medium heat.
2. Melt butter on top of the hot griddle.
3. Add tomato and chili pepper and sauté for 2 minutes.
4. In a bowl, whisk eggs with cilantro, cream, pepper, and salt.
5. Pour egg mixture over tomato and chili pepper and stir until egg is set.
6. Garnish with scallions and serve.

Nutrition Info: (Per Serving): Calories 355 ;Fat 33 g ;Carbohydrates 3 g ;Sugar 1.7 g ;Protein 12 g ;Cholesterol 401 mg

Bacon And Gruyere Omelet

Servings: 2
Cooking Time: 15 Minutes
Ingredients:

- 6 eggs, beaten
- 6 strips bacon
- 1/4 lb gruyere, shredded
- 1 teaspoon black pepper
- 1 teaspoon salt
- 1 tablespoon chives, finely chopped
- vegetable oil

Directions:

1. Add salt to the beaten eggs and set aside for 10 minutes.
2. Heat your griddle to medium heat and add the bacon strips. Cook until most of the fat has rendered, but bacon is still flexible. Remove the bacon from the griddle and place on paper towels.
3. Once the bacon has drained, chop into small pieces.
4. Add the eggs to the griddle in two even pools. Cook until the bottom of the eggs starts to firm up. Add the gruyere to the eggs and cook until the cheese has started to melt and the eggs are just starting to brown.
5. Add the bacon pieces and use a spatula to turn one half of the omelet onto the other half. Remove from the griddle, season with pepper and chives and serve.

Nutrition Info: Calories: 734, Sodium: 855 mg, Dietary Fiber: 0.3g, Fat: 55.3.g, Carbs: 2.8g Protein: 54.8g

Blistered Green Beans

Servings: 4 Slices
Cooking Time: 10 Minutes
Ingredients:

- 1 pound haricots verts or green beans, trimmed
- 2 tablespoons vegetable oil
- Juice of 1 lemon

- Pinch red pepper flakes
- Flaky sea salt
- Freshly ground black pepper

Directions:

1. Preheat the griddle to medium high.
2. While the unit is preheating, in a medium bowl, toss the green beans in oil until evenly coated.
3. Place the green beans on the Grill and grill for 8 to 10 minutes, tossing frequently until blistered on all sides.
4. When cooking is complete, place the green beans on a large serving platter. Squeeze lemon juice over the green beans, top with red pepper flakes, and season with sea salt and black pepper.

Nutrition Info: (Per serving): Calories: 100kcal; Fat: 7g; Carbs: 10g; Protein: 2g

Pigs In A Blanket

Servings: 4
Cooking Time: 10 Minutes
Ingredients:

- Buttermilk Pancake batter
- 8 breakfast sausage links

Directions:

1. Preparing the Ingredients.
2. Make the buttermilk pancake batter.
3. Bring the griddle grill to medium-high heat.
4. Grilling
5. Cook the breakfast sausage links until they are completely cooked through, with the juices running clear, or when they reach an internal temperature of 165°F, then set aside and keep warm.
6. Follow the directions for making buttermilk pancakes. Using your spatula, coax the pancake to roll around the sausage link like a blanket. Allow to continue Grilling with the sausage in the middle until the pancake is fully cooked.

Classic Buttermilk Pancakes

Servings: 4
Cooking Time: 10 Minutes
Ingredients:

- 2 cups all purpose flour
- 3 tablespoons sugar

- 1 1/2 teaspoons baking powder
- 1 1/2 teaspoons baking soda
- 1 1/4 teaspoons salt
- 2 1/2 cups buttermilk
- 2 eggs
- 3 tablespoons unsalted butter, melted
- vegetable oil

Directions:

1. In a large bowl, combine the flour, sugar, baking soda, baking powder, and salt.
2. Stir in the buttermilk, eggs, and butter, and mix until combined but not totally smooth.
3. Heat your griddle to medium heat and add a small amount of oil. Using a paper towel, spread the oil over the griddle in a very thin layer.
4. Use a ladle to pour the batter onto the griddle allowing a few inches between pancakes.
5. When the surface of the pancakes is bubbly, flip and cook a few additional minutes. Remove the pancakes from the griddle and serve immediately with butter and maple syrup.

Nutrition Info: Calories: 432, Sodium: 458 mg, Dietary Fiber: 1.7g, Fat: 12.8.g, Carbs: 65.1g Protein: 14.4g

Best Johnny Cakes

Servings: 2
Cooking Time: 10 Minutes
Ingredients:

- 2 eggs
- 1⅓ cups milk
- 1 tablespoon honey
- ¼ cup Grilling oil
- 1½ cups all-purpose flour
- ½ cup fine cornmeal
- 4 teaspoons baking powder
- 1 tablespoon sugar
- 1 teaspoon salt

Directions:

1. Preparing the Ingredients.
2. Beat the eggs, milk, honey, and oil in a medium bowl until frothy. Combine the flour, cornmeal, baking powder, sugar, and salt in a large bowl and mix to combine.

3. Add the wet ingredients to the dry ingredients and mix until well-incorporated and free of clumps. Let sit for 20 Minutes while your grill heats up.

4. Bring the griddle grill to medium-high heat. Oil the griddle and allow it to heat until the oil is shimmering but not smoking.

5. Grilling

6. Pour about ¼ cup of batter onto the griddle grill for each pancake. The pancakes should slowly begin to form bubbles. After 2 to 4 Minutes, when the bubbles pop and leave small holes, flip the pancakes. Cook for an additional 2 Minutes.

Broccoli Omelet

Servings: 2
Cooking Time: 10 Minutes
Ingredients:

- 4 eggs
- 1 cup broccoli, chopped and cooked
- 1 tbsp olive oil
- 1/4 tsp pepper
- 1/2 tsp salt

Directions:

1. In a bowl, beat eggs with pepper, and salt.

2. Preheat the griddle to medium heat. Add oil to the griddle top.

3. Pour broccoli and egg mixture onto the hot griddle top and cook until set. Flip omelet and cook until lightly golden brown.

4. Serve and enjoy.

Nutrition Info: (Per Serving): Calories 203 ;Fat 16 g ;Carbohydrates 4 g ;Sugar 1.5 g ;Protein 12 g ;Cholesterol 327 mg

Potato Pancakes

Servings: 2
Cooking Time: 10 Minutes
Ingredients:

- 2 eggs
- ¼ cup milk
- 1½ cups russet potato, peeled and shredded
- ¼ cup all-purpose flour
- ¼ cup finely diced onion
- ¼ cup finely chopped green onion
- 1 teaspoon baking powder
- 1 teaspoon salt
- 1 teaspoon pepper
- Grilling oil, as needed

Directions:

1. Preparing the Ingredients.

2. In a large bowl, Whisk the eggs and milk until frothy. Add the remaining ingredients and mix to combine. The batter should be moist throughout but not pooling with liquid. Allow to rest for 20 Minutes while the grill heats up.

3. Bring the griddle grill to medium-high heat.

4. Add a thin coat of oil to the Grilling surface, and when it begins to shimmer, add about ¼ cup of potato pancake batter to the griddle for each pancake.

5. Grilling

6. Press the batter to flatten and cook each side for 3 to 4 Minutes until golden brown.

Classic Eggs Benedict

Servings: 2
Cooking Time: 10 Minutes
Ingredients:

- 1 medium red or green bell pepper
- 2 English muffins
- 2 eggs
- 4 slices Canadian bacon
- ½ cup very finely shredded Jarlsberg cheese
- butter, as needed

Directions:

1. Preparing the Ingredients.

2. Bring the griddle grill to medium heat. Cut the uneven bottom off the bell pepper, then cut two rings of pepper about ½ inch thick.

3. Grilling

4. Coat the griddle with a good amount of butter. Separate the English muffins and place the uncut-sides on the griddle to begin warming. Place the bell pepper rings on the griddle and cook for 2 Minutes. Flip the peppers, then flip the English muffins to heat the other sides.

5. Crack an egg and carefully drop it into one of the bell pepper rings. Scoot the other pepper ring close by and repeat with the second egg. Using a cover

that's just bigger than the peppers, cover the eggs and allow them to cook for 1 minute.

6.   While the eggs are Grilling, warm the Canadian bacon on the grilling surface.

7.   Remove the cover from the eggs and squirt water around the grilling surface very close to the eggs, and immediately cover the eggs again to capture the steam and assist with Grilling the whites and yolks. Cook for another minute, then cover each of the eggs with half of the cheese. The finer the cheese is grated, the more quickly it will melt, so I use a very fine grater or even a Microplane. Squirt the perimeter of the eggs again and cover to catch the steam, allowing the cheese to melt.

8.   Remove the English muffins from the griddle and Place 2 slices of Canadian bacon on top of each. Uncover the eggs, and using a spatula, remove the pepper ring containing the egg and slide it onto the Canadian bacon.

Grilled Fruit Salad With Honey-lime Glaze

Servings: 4
Cooking Time: 4 Minutes
Ingredients:
- 1/2 pound strawberries, washed, hulled and halved
- 1 (9 oz.) can pineapple chunks, drained, juice reserved
- 2 peaches, pitted and sliced
- 6 tbsps. honey, divided
- 1 tbsp. freshly squeezed lime juice

Directions:
1.   Preheat your griddle to medium high.
2.   While the unit is preheating, combine the strawberries, pineapple, and peaches in a large bowl with 3 tablespoons of honey. Toss to coat evenly.
3.   Place the fruit on the grill top. Gently press the fruit down to maximize grill marks. Grill for 4 minutes without flipping.
4.   Meanwhile, in a small bowl, combine the remaining 3 tablespoons of honey, lime juice, and 1 tablespoon of reserved pineapple juice.
5.   When cooking is complete, place the fruit in a large bowl and toss with the honey mixture. Serve immediately.

Nutrition Info: (Per serving): Calories: 178kcal; fat: 1g; Carbs: 47g; Protein: 2g

Classic Steak And Eggs

Servings: 4
Cooking Time: 10 Minutes
Ingredients:
- 1 pound Sirloin, cut into 4 1/2-inch thick pieces
- 8 large eggs
- 3 tablespoons vegetable oil
- salt and black pepper

Directions:
1.   Preheat griddle to medium-high heat on one side and medium heat on the other.
2.   Season the steaks with a generous amount of salt and pepper.
3.   Place steaks on the medium high side and cook for 3 minutes and add the oil to the medium heat side.
4.   Flip the steaks and crack the eggs onto the medium heat side of the griddle.
5.   After 3 minutes remove the steaks from the griddle and allow to rest 5 minutes. Finish cooking the eggs and place two eggs and one piece of steak on each plate to serve. Season the eggs with a pinch of salt and pepper.

Nutrition Info: Calories: 444, Sodium: 215 mg, Dietary Fiber: 0g, Fat: 27.2g, Carbs: 0.8g Protein: 47g

Classic French Toast

Servings: 4
Cooking Time: 10 Minutes
Ingredients:
- 6 eggs, beaten
- 1/4 cup "half and half" or heavy cream
- 8 slices thick cut white or sourdough bread
- 2 tablespoons sugar
- 1 tablespoon cinnamon
- 1 teaspoon salt
- butter
- powdered sugar
- maple syrup

Directions:
1.   Heat your griddle to medium heat.

2. In a large bowl, combine the eggs, cream, sugar, cinnamon, and salt. Mix well until smooth.

3. Lightly grease the griddle with butter or vegetable oil.

4. Dip each slice of bread in the mixture until well saturated with egg then place onto the griddle.

5. When the French toast has begun to brown, flip and cook until the other side has browned as well. About four minutes.

6. Remove the French toast from the griddle, dust with powdered sugar, and serve with warm maple syrup.

Nutrition Info: Calories: 332, Sodium: 593 mg, Dietary Fiber: 2.4g, Fat: 10.5.g, Carbs: 44.2g Protein: 16g

Tomato Scrambled Egg

Servings: 2

Cooking Time: 5 Minutes

Ingredients:

- 2 eggs, lightly beaten
- 2 tbsp fresh basil, chopped
- 1 tbsp olive oil
- 1/2 tomato, chopped
- Pepper
- Salt

Directions:

1. Preheat the griddle to medium heat.

2. Add oil on top of the griddle.

3. Add tomatoes and cook until softened.

4. Whisk eggs with basil, pepper, and salt.

5. Pour egg mixture on top of tomatoes and cook until eggs are set.

6. Serve and enjoy.

Nutrition Info: (Per Serving): Calories 125 ;Fat 12 g ;Carbohydrates 1 g ;Sugar 0.8 g ;Protein 5.8 g ;Cholesterol 164 mg

Upside-down Plum Cake

Servings: 8

Cooking Time: 30 Minutes

Ingredients:

- 8 tablespoons (1 stick) butter
- ½ cup brown sugar
- 1½ pounds small ripe red plums, halved and pitted (if the plums are large and/or hard, slice them to make sure they cook through)
- 1 cup buttermilk
- 2 eggs
- ½ cup granulated sugar
- 2 cups all-purpose flour
- 1 teaspoon baking soda
- ¼ teaspoon salt

Directions:

1. Preparing the Ingredients.

2. Melt 4 tablespoons (½ stick) of the butter in a 9- or 10-inch cast-iron skillet over low heat; remove from the heat. Sprinkle the brown sugar evenly over the bottom of the pan and arrange the plums in a single layer over the brown sugar, cut side down.

3. Melt the remaining 4 tablespoons (½ stick) butter. Add it to the buttermilk, eggs, and granulated sugar in a medium-sized bowl and Beat until foamy. In a large bowl, Beat the flour, baking soda, and salt. (You can make the cake ahead to this point. If not grilling within 30 Minutes, refrigerate the buttermilk mixture.)

4. If using a Griddle, heat it for medium-high direct

5. Grilling

6. The grill temperature should be 500° to 600°F; it could mean all the burners are on medium or medium-low, depending on your particular grill.

7. When you're ready to bake, gradually add the egg mixture to the dry ingredients and mix until well incorporated. Spoon the batter over the plums and spread gently with a spatula until it's evenly thick.

8. Place the skillet on the grill directly. Bake for 10 Minutes, then check. If the cake seems to be browning too fast, turn the heat off under the pan and turn it up on the other burners on a Griddle. Keep checking every few Minutes until the top of the cake is golden brown and a toothpick inserted into the center comes out clean, 5 to 15 Minutes more, depending on how hot it is. Carefully transfer the skillet to a rack and let the cake cool for no more than 5 Minutes. Run a knife around the edge to loosen the cake. Place a serving plate on top of the skillet and carefully invert the hot pan over the plate. The cake should fall out. If it sticks, turn it right side up again, run the knife along the edge again, and use a spatula to gently lift around the edge. Invert again and tap.

Remove any stuck fruit from the bottom of the pan with a knife and fit it back into any gaps on the top of the cake.

Simple French Crepes

Servings: 4
Cooking Time: 15 Minutes
Ingredients:
- 1 1/4 cups flour
- 3/4 cup whole milk
- 1/2 cup water
- 2 eggs
- 3 tablespoons unsalted butter, melted
- 1 teaspoon vanilla
- 2 tablespoon sugar

Directions:
1. In a large bowl, add all the ingredients and mix with a whisk. Make sure the batter is smooth. Rest for 1 hour.
2. Heat your Blackstone Griddle to medium heat and add a thin layer of butter. Add about ¼ cup of the batter. Using a crepe spreading tool, form your crepe and cook for 1-2 minutes. Use your Crepe Spatula and flip. Cook for another minute.
3. Top with Nutella and strawberries for a sweet crepe, or top with scrambled eggs and black forest ham for a savory crepe

Nutrition Info: Calories: 303, Sodium: 112mg, Dietary Fiber: 1.1g, Fat: 12.7g, Carbs: 38.2g Protein: 8.4g

Lebanese Bread

Servings: 8
Cooking Time: 1½ Hours
Ingredients:
- 1 tablespoon instant yeast
- 2 teaspoons salt
- 1 teaspoon sugar
- 1 cup warm water, plus more as needed
- 3 cups all-purpose flour, plus more as needed
- 3 tablespoons za'atar (to make your own
- 3 tablespoons good-quality olive oil

Directions:
1. Preparing the Ingredients.

2. Beat the yeast, salt, sugar, and 1 cup water together in a large bowl. Add the flour and mix with a heavy spoon until the mixture can be formed into a ball; it should be slightly sticky. If it's dry, add more water 1 tablespoon at a time until you get the right consistency; in the unlikely event that the mixture is too sticky, add flour 1 tablespoon at a time. Turn the dough out onto a lightly floured work surface; knead a few times until smooth. Place the dough in a bowl and cover with plastic wrap; let rise until it doubles in size, about 1 hour.
3. Heat a Griddle for medium-high heat.
4. Grilling
5. Make sure the grates are clean.
6. Beat the za'atar into the oil in a small bowl.
7. When the dough is ready, transfer it to a well-floured work surface and knead for a few Minutes, until smooth and pliable. Cut into 8 equal-sized pieces. Roll each piece into an oval roughly 6 to 8 inches long and 3 to 4 inches wide. Stack them between wax paper or parchment and bring the breads to the grill along with the za'atar oil, a brush, and a baking sheet. Working in batches, just before Grilling, brush the za'atar oil over the breads to within ½ inch of the edge; make sure to get plenty of the sesame seeds and thyme that are suspended in the oil.
8. One at a time, use your hands to pick up an oval by the long ends and drop it onto the grate directly, with the long side perpendicular to the grates. Cook until the dough bubbles up on top, the outer edges start to brown, and the bottom develops grill marks; depending on how hot it is, this will take 1½ to 3 Minutes. Start checking at 1½ Minutes, then every 30 seconds after that. Use a spatula to transfer the breads to the baking sheet and repeat with the remaining dough and za'atar oil. Serve warm or within several hours.

Naan Bread

Servings: 4
Cooking Time: 2½ Hours
Ingredients:
- ¼ cup yogurt
- 2 tablespoons good-quality vegetable oil, plus more for the bowl
- 1 tablespoon sugar
- 2¼ teaspoons (1 package) instant yeast

- 3½ cups all-purpose flour, plus more as needed
- ½ cup whole wheat flour
- 2 teaspoons salt
- 1½ cups warm water, plus more as needed
- 6 tablespoons (¾ stick) butter, melted and still warm

Directions:

1. Preparing the Ingredients.
2. Beat the yogurt, oil, sugar, and yeast together. Mix the flours and salt together in a large bowl. Add the yogurt mixture and combine. Add the water ½ cup at a time, stirring until the mixture comes together in a cohesive but sticky dough; you may need to add another tablespoon or 2 water.
3. Turn the dough out onto a floured work surface and knead by hand for a minute or so to form a smooth dough. Shape into a round ball, Place in a lightly oiled bowl, and cover with plastic wrap. Let rise until doubled in size, 1 to 2 hours. Or you can let the dough rise in the refrigerator for up to 8 hours.
4. Punch the dough down. Using as much flour as necessary to keep the dough from sticking to the work surface or your hands, roll it into a snake about 2 inches in diameter, then tear into 12 equal-sized balls. Space the balls out on the work surface. Cover with plastic wrap or a clean, damp dish towel and let rest for 10 Minutes. Roll each dough ball into an oval roughly 6 to 8 inches long and 3 to 4 inches wide.
5. Heat a Griddle for hot direct
6. Grilling
7. Make sure the grates are clean. Have the melted butter handy.
8. Working in batches, Place the naan on the grill directly. If the grill temperature is 600°F or above, it will only take 20 to 30 seconds for the first side to brown. It should smell toasty, not burning. the visible side should be bubbled. Quickly turn with tongs. The other side will take about the same time or a little less to cook. When you grab it with tongs, the bread should feel firm and springy, and both sides should be browned in spots, with a little charring. Transfer to a platter and immediately brush with the butter. Repeat with the remaining naan and butter and serve as soon as possible.

French Toast With Ice Cream

Servings: 4
Cooking Time: 10 Minutes
Ingredients:

- 1 cup melted vanilla ice cream
- 3 eggs
- 1 teaspoon vanilla extract
- pinch of ground cinnamon
- 8 slices Texas toast or other thick-cut bread
- Grilling oil, as needed

Directions:

1. Preparing the Ingredients.
2. Combine the melted ice cream, eggs, vanilla extract, and cinnamon in a bowl wide enough for the bread to be easily dipped into. Mix very well or until frothy.
3. Bring the griddle grill to medium-high heat and coat the surface with oil. When the oil begins to shimmer, dip each side of the bread into the egg batter so it lightly coats each side. Allow any additional batter to drain back into the bowl.
4. Grilling
5. Place the bread on the griddle. Cook for 3 to 4 Minutes per side, or until the French toast is golden brown. Repeat with the remaining ingredients.

Strawberry, Banana, Crepes

Servings: 2
Cooking Time: 10 Minutes
Ingredients:

- 6 tablespoons hazelnut-chocolate spread
- 2 prepared crepes
- 8 large strawberries, sliced
- 1 banana, sliced
- powdered sugar

Directions:

1. Preparing the Ingredients.
2. Spread half the hazelnut-chocolate spread on each of the crepes and divide the fruit evenly as a topping.
3. Fold the crepes over the filling and garnish with powdered sugar.

Maple-balsamic Boneless Pork Chops

Servings: 4 Slices
Cooking Time: 10 Minutes
Ingredients:

- 1 tbsp. extra virgin olive oil
- 4 (4-oz.) boneless pork chops
- Salt and black pepper, to taste
- 1/2 cup balsamic vinegar
- 2-1/2 tbsps. real maple syrup

Directions:
1. Prepare griddle for medium heat. Lightly oil.
2. Season pork chops on each side with salt and pepper, to taste, and add to the pre-heated griddle. Brown pork chops on each side, approximately 3 minutes per side. Remove pork chops from pan and set aside on a rimmed dish.
3. Place small aluminum roasting pan to your flat top. Heat this heat zone to high. Add balsamic vinegar and maple syrup and bring to a boil, stirring constantly.
4. Reduce heat to medium and cook mixture until it is reduced to about 1/3 of its original volume. When ready, the glaze will become thick and syrupy. (Do not overcook or the mixture will become hard and sticky).
5. Transfer chops to a serving platter or individual serving plate and drizzle with pan sauce. Serve immediately with griddled Brussels sprouts or your choice of sides.
Nutrition Info: (Per serving):Calories 351.2kcal; protein 25.7 g; carbs 33.2 g; fat 20g

Fennel-orange Slaw

Servings: 4
Cooking Time: 55 Minutes
Ingredients:

- ½ cup rice vinegar
- ¼ cup sugar
- 1 small red onion, halved, thinly sliced, and pulled apart
- 2 pounds fennel
- 2 tablespoons good-quality olive oil, plus more for brushing
- 3 navel oranges
- 1 teaspoon minced fresh rosemary
- Salt and pepper

Directions:
1. Preparing the Ingredients.
2. Place the vinegar and sugar in a small nonreactive saucepan and bring to a boil. Remove from the heat, add the onion, and mix to combine. Or you can do this earlier in the day, cover, and let sit at room temperature.
3. Heat a Griddle for medium heat. Grilling. Make sure the grates are clean.
4. Trim the fennel bulbs, reserving the feathery fronds. Cut the fennel in half from stalk end to base; brush with some oil. Cut the peel from the oranges with a small knife, deep enough to remove the white pith. Slice the oranges across into ¼-inch rounds, then cut the rounds into wedges. Place in a large bowl.
5. Place the fennel on the grill directly.
6. Grilling.
7. Turning once, until the fennel is crisp-tender and browned or charred in spots, 3 to 5 Minutes per side. Transfer to a cutting board and thinly slice across into crescents. Add to the oranges. Use a slotted spoon to transfer the onion to the bowl; reserve the brine. Mince enough fennel fronds to make 2 tablespoons.
8. Add the oil, 1 tablespoon of the brine, the rosemary, the minced fronds, and some salt and pepper. Toss to coat, taste and adjust the seasoning, and serve. Or prepare the slaw up to a day ahead, cover, and refrigerate.

Chicken Ranch Pizza

Servings: 6
Ingredients:

- 1 pizza dough
- 2 cups cheddar, shredded
- 2 cups cooked rotisserie chicken, shredded
- 4 strips bacon, cooked crispy & crumbled
- ¼ cup scallions ½ cup ranch dressing

Directions:
1. Preparing the Ingredients.

2. Arrange pizza dough to fit onto the Grill Pan
3. Grilling
4. Preheat the oven to 400° F. On medium heat, grill pizza on both sides until golden.
5. Sprinkle shredded cheddar onto the dough. Top with chicken, bacon, and scallions.
6. Place the Grill Pan into the oven. Bake until the cheese is melted and the dough is cooked through. Spry ranch dressing over the pizza immediately before serving.Make it a club by topping with chopped lettuce, tomato and avocado!

Creamy Mustard-garlic Potato Salad

Servings: 4
Cooking Time: 40 Minutes
Ingredients:
- 1½ pounds potatoes, peeled if you like, cut into bite-sized pieces
- Salt
- ½ cup mayonnaise (to make your own
- 3 tablespoons white wine vinegar or cider vinegar
- 1 tablespoon Dijon mustard
- 1 teaspoon minced garlic, or more to taste
- ¼ cup chopped scallions
- Pepper

Directions:
1. Preparing the Ingredients.
2. Place the potatoes in a pot with enough water to cover them and add a large pinch salt. Bring to a boil, then lower the heat so the water bubbles gently.
3. Grilling
4. The potatoes until fork-tender but not at all mushy or breaking apart, about 15 Minutes. Drain, rinse under cold running water, then drain again.
5. Beat the mayonnaise, vinegar, mustard, garlic, and scallions together in a medium-sized bowl. Add the potatoes and toss or fold gently (you don't want the cubes to break up) until they're coated. Taste and adjust the seasoning. Serve right away, or refrigerate in an airtight container for up to 3 days.

Crispy Asian-seared Salmon

Servings: 2

Cooking Time: 15 Minutes
Ingredients:
- 2 (4-ounce) salmon fillets
- ¾ cup Asian Griddle Sauce, plus more as needed
- Grilling oil, as needed
- salt and pepper, to taste

Directions:
1. Preparing the Ingredients.
2. Wash the salmon fillets and pat dry. Check for pin bones by placing salmon skin-side down on a cutting board and gently running your fingers across the thicker parts of the fillet. If you feel any bones, use a pair of tweezers to remove them before Grilling.
3. Flip the salmon over, skin-side up. Typically, the salmon will resemble the shape of an airplane wing: thick, oval-round on one end, and tapering off to a very thin side on the other end. Make three or four ¼-inch cuts across the skin on the thickest part of the filet. This will allow the filet to cook a bit more evenly and with less curling when it is on the griddle. Season both sides of the filet with salt and pepper and make sure to get some seasoning into the areas where you scored the skin.
4. Grilling
5. Bring the griddle grill to medium-high heat and add Grilling oil to the surface. When the oil is shimmering, place the salmon skin-side down and cook for 3 or 4 Minutes without disturbing. This develops a crispy crust on the salmon skin that many people find quite delicious.
6. When you are ready to flip, place the spatula on the griddle grill at an aggressive 15-degree angle and scrape under the skin to release and flip the salmon.
7. Shake the Asian Griddle Sauce well and add about ¾ cup to the griddle near the salmon. Slide the salmon into the sauce, cover it, and allow it to steam cook for another 5 Minutes. If desired, flip the salmon an additional time and allow it to bathe in the Asian Griddle Sauce before plating.

Baby Potatoes With Sea Salt

Servings: 4
Cooking Time: 30 Minutes
Ingredients:
- 1½ pounds fingerling or baby potatoes

- 3 tablespoons good-quality olive oil
- 1 tablespoon coarse sea salt

Directions:
1. Preparing the Ingredients.
2. Heat a Griddle for medium heat.
3. Grilling
4. Make sure the grates are clean.
5. Place the potatoes in a large bowl. Spry them with the oil and toss to coat completely. Sprinkle with the salt and toss again.
6. Place the potatoes on the grill directly. Cook turning them once or twice, until a knife inserted in the center of a potato goes through without any resistance, 10 to 20 Minutes total. Transfer to a platter and serve.
7. Fingerling or Baby Potatoes with Rosemary and Lemon Zest
8. I love lemon with potatoes: When you season the potatoes, add pepper. Toss the grilled potatoes with 1 tablespoon chopped fresh rosemary and the grated zest of 1 lemon before serving.
9. Fingerling or Baby Potatoes with Oregano and Garlic
10. The perfect side for grilled steak or chicken: When you season the potatoes, add pepper. Toss the grilled potatoes with 1 tablespoon chopped fresh oregano and 2 teaspoons minced garlic before serving.
11. Fingerling or Baby Potatoes with Grill-Roasted Garlic
12. For a mellow garlic flavor: When you season the potatoes, add pepper. Toss the grilled potatoes with 2 tablespoons mashed Grill-Roasted Garlic, or more to taste, before serving.

Easy Chickpea Falafel

Servings: 4
Cooking Time: 15 Minutes
Ingredients:
- 1 (16-ounce) can chickpeas, drained
- ¾ cup diced sweet onion
- ¼ cup diced shallot
- 2 tablespoons freshly chopped parsley
- 4 cloves garlic, minced
- 1 teaspoon ground cumin
- 1 teaspoon paprika
- 1 teaspoon olive oil
- 1 teaspoon salt
- 1 teaspoon pepper
- ¼ cup all-purpose flour
- 1 teaspoon baking powder
- Grilling oil, as needed

Directions:
1. Preparing the Ingredients.
2. Combine all the ingredients except the flour and baking powder in a food processor or blender. Mixuntil smooth with some small chunks remaining, scraping the sides of the bowl 2 to 3 times to make sure all of the ingredients are incorporated.
3. Transfer the falafel mix to a medium bowl. Sift and then mix in the flour and baking powder. Mix by hand until the mixture absorbs the flour and becomes firmer. Cover tightly and allow to rest in the refrigerator for at least an hour.
4. Bring the griddle grill to medium heat and form the falafel into 4 patties just under 1 inch thick.
5. Grilling
6. Add a generous amount of oil to your Grilling surface and allow it to heat until shimmering. Place the patties in the hot oil and allow to cook 3 to 4 Minutes, covered. Flip and cook, covered, for an additional 3 to 4 Minutes, until heated through and a golden crust has formed.

Asian Style Beef Broccoli Recipe

Servings: 2-4 Slices
Cooking Time: 10 Minutes
Ingredients:
- 1/2 lb. sukiyaki cut beef (very thin across the grain slices)
- 3 cups Chinese broccoli
- 1/3 cup brown sugar
- 1/3 cup water
- 1/3 cup soy sauce
- 3 tbsps. cooking oil
- 2 tbsps. browned chopped garlic (you may use garlic flakes)
- 2 tbsps. sesame oil
- 1/2 tsp. red chili flakes
- 1/2 tsp. freshly grounded black pepper

Directions:

1. Get all of your ingredients together.

2. Prepare griddle for medium heat. Lightly oil. Place on broccoli on flat top. Cover with basting cover. Add a little water to the surface before you cover to steam Chinese broccoli until it is done but not soggy. It is important to retain the bright green color for the visual appeal of the meal; plus the crunchy texture of the cooked vegetable add a certain freshness to the dish.

3. Cook the beef in the cooking oil until browned. It would only take 3 minutes in medium to high heat because the beef is very thinly cut.

4. Once the beef has been cooked and browned, add in the water, soy sauce, brown sugar, half of the garlic, the red chili flakes and black pepper. Simmer for 3 minutes.

5. On a serving dish, arrange the Chinese broccoli and spoon the cooked beef and the sauce over it. Top with the rest of the garlic flakes and drizzle in the sesame oil.

6. Serve and enjoy! This recipe serves 2-4 individuals depending if the dish is to be served as a side dish or a main dish. It's a visual treat for sure!

Nutrition Info: (Per serving):calories 331.4kcal; protein 21.7 g; carbs 13.3 g; fat 15g.

Mediterranean Pork Chops

Servings: 6

Ingredients:

- 6 pork chops, thick cut ¼ cup olive oil
- 1 tbsp. sea salt
- 1 tsp. ground black pepper

Directions:

1. Preparing the Ingredients.

2. Rub pork chops with olive oil, sea salt, and pepper.

3. Grilling

4. Grill about 5-7 Minutes per side or until internal temperature reaches 165° F. In a bowl, combine all salad ingredients. Toss. Serve pork chops with salad and your favorite side dishes. Salad ½ cup kalamata olives 1 clove garlic, peeled & minced 1 pint cherry tomatoes, quartered 4 cups feta cheese 3 tbsp. red wine vinegar 1 sprig oregano, fresh ¼ cup extra virgin olive oil 1 cup cannellini beans

Thai-style Coleslaw

Servings: 8

Cooking Time: 20 Minutes

Ingredients:

- 1 small head cabbage (1 pound)
- ¼ cup fresh lime juice
- ¼ cup fish sauce
- 1 tablespoon minced garlic
- 1 tablespoon sugar
- 1 small red chile (like Thai), chopped, or ½ teaspoon red chile flakes or more to taste
- ¼ cup chopped fresh mint

Directions:

1. Preparing the Ingredients.

2. Discard any discolored outer leaves from the cabbage, cut it into quarters, and remove the core. Cut across into thin ribbons or shred on the largest holes of a box grater or in a food processor with the shredding disk.

3. Beat the lime juice, fish sauce, garlic, sugar, and chile together in a large bowl. Add the shredded cabbage and mint and toss with the dressing until completely coated. Serve immediately, or cover and refrigerate until you're ready to serve.

Savory Applesauce On The Grill

Servings: 2

Cooking Time: 45 Minutes

Ingredients:

- 1½ pounds whole apples
- Salt

Directions:

1. Preparing the Ingredients.

2. Heat a Griddle for medium heat.

3. Grilling

4. Make sure the grates are clean.

5. Place the apples on the grill directly. Cook until the fruit feels soft when gently squeezed with tongs, 10 to 20 Minutes total, depending on their size. Transfer to a cutting board and let sit until cool enough to touch.

6. Cut the flesh from around the core of each apple; discard the cores. Place the chunks in a blender or

food processor and process until smooth, or Place them in a bowl and purée with an immersion blender until as chunky or smooth as you like. Add a generous pinch of salt, then taste and adjust the seasoning. Serve or refrigerate in an airtight container for up to 3 days.

Beef Honey Curry Stir Fry Recipe

Servings: 3-4 Slices
Cooking Time: 10 Minutes
Ingredients:
- 1/2 lb. sukiyaki cut beef
- 1/2 cup honey
- 1/2 cup soy sauce
- 4 tbsps. curry powder
- 4 tbsps. oil
- 1 tsp. ground black pepper
- 1 medium sized red onion, sliced
- 1 medium sized red bell pepper, sliced into strips
- 1 medium sized green bell pepper, sliced into strips
- 1 medium sized yellow bell pepper, sliced into strips
- Roasting pan

Directions:
1. Prepare all the ingredients that you'll need.
2. Marinate the beef with marinade made of soy sauce, curry powder, honey and ground black pepper and let it stand for 15 minutes.
3. Prepare your flat top to medium high heat. Oil and sauté the red bell pepper, green bell pepper, red onion and yellow bell pepper for a few minutes (usually just a little over a minute), taking care that the vegetables are cooked but not wilted. They should remain crunchy for great texture. Take the cooked vegetables off the pan and set aside.
4. Remove beef from marinate mixed and place on griddle until halfway cooked. Remove and place in roasting pan.
5. Place roasting pan on griddle and add in the remaining half of the oil and marinade and cook the beef together with the marinade over medium heat until the sauce thickens, and the beef is cooked

through. This only takes 5-7 minutes. Turn off the heat.
6. Toss the cooked vegetables with the beef in the pain to coat it with some of the sauce and bring all flavors together. Serve over steaming hot rice, mashed potato, or even pasta! This recipe makes for about 3-4 servings.
Nutrition Info: (Per serving): Calories: 473.68kcal Carbs: 16.02g Protein: 24.21g Fat: 34.34g

From-scratch Baked Beans

Servings: 4
Cooking Time: 4 Hours
Ingredients:
- 1 pound dried navy, great Northern, or other dried white beans (limas, pintos, and red beans also work), picked over, rinsed, and soaked for 6 to 12 hours in water to cover
- 8 ounces salt pork or slab bacon
- ½ cup molasses, or to taste
- 2 teaspoons dry mustard or 2 tablespoons Dijon mustard, or more to taste
- Salt and pepper

Directions:
1. Preparing the Ingredients.
2. Drain the beans, Place in a large ovenproof pot, and add water to cover the beans by 2 inches. Bring to a boil, reduce the heat so the water is gently bubbling, partially cover the pot, and
3. Grilling.
4. The beans just until they begin to become tender, 15 to 30 Minutes depending on the bean. Drain the beans, reserving the Grilling liquid; no need to rinse the pot.
5. Heat the oven to 300°F. Cube or slice the salt pork or bacon and Place it in the bottom of the pot you used to cook the beans. Cover the meat with the beans and add the molasses and mustard. Add enough of the reserved liquid to cover the bean mixture by about an inch. (Add boiling water if there's not enough.) Mix to combine.
6. Bake, uncovered, for an hour. After that, check and mix every half hour or so, adding more water if necessary to keep everything covered. After about 3

hours, taste and adjust the seasoning with salt and pepper, as well as more mustard or molasses.

7.   When the beans are very tender, fish out the meat and Place it on top of the beans; raise the heat to 400°F. Bake until the pork browns a bit and the beans are bubbly, about 10 Minutes. Serve hot.

Scallops And Asparagus Tips

Servings: 2
Cooking Time: 15 Minutes
Ingredients:

- 2 cups asparagus tips
- 8 large dry scallops
- White Wine Griddle Sauce, as needed
- butter, as needed
- Grilling oil, as needed
- salt and pepper, to taste

Directions:
1.   Preparing the Ingredients.
2.   Bring the griddle grill to medium-high heat.
3.   Grilling
4.   Coat the griddle with Grilling oil, and when it begins to shimmer, place the asparagus on the grill. Allow to cook for 2 Minutes, stirring frequently.
5.   Cover the asparagus and place the scallops on the griddle with plenty of room between them. Scallops will only cook for 2 Minutes per side, so set a timer.
6.   Just before you flip the scallops, give the asparagus a squirt of the White Wine Griddle Sauce and add a pat of butter. Flip the scallops and allow them to cook for another 2 Minutes until done. Season with salt and pepper to taste.
7.   Serve the asparagus alongside the scallops.

Skirt Steak Sandwich

Servings: 4
Ingredients:

- 1 lb. skirt steak
- 1 shallot, peeled & minced
- 3 tbsp. balsamic vinegar ¼ cup olive oil ½ tsp. sea salt

Directions:
1.   Preparing the Ingredients.

2.   In a shallow pan, marinate steak with shallots, balsamic vinegar, olive oil, sea salt, and pepper for 1 hour. Combine tapenade ingredients in a bowl. Set aside.
3.   Grilling
4.   Grill the steak to desired temperature. Let rest 10 Minutes before slicing. Assemble sliced steak andtapenade open-face on focaccia. Serve with your favorite side dish. ½ tsp. course ground black pepper 3 slices focaccia, grilled. Tomato Red Onion Tapenade ¼ cup olive oil 2 tbsp. red wine vinegar 1 clove garlic, peeled & minced ½ tsp. sea salt ¼ tsp. ground black pepper 3 roma tomatoes, chopped ¼ red onion, diced 6 basil leaves, chopped. Don't forget to let your steak rest for 5-10 Minutes so it stays juicy. It's also important to slice the meat against the grain. For an extra special treat, add a little crumbled Gorgonzola cheese, I promise you won't be disappointed!

Mushroom Bruschetta

Servings: 2
Cooking Time: 15 Minutes
Ingredients:

- 2 large portobello mushrooms, with stems
- 2 tbsp. olive oil
- 1 clove garlic, peeled & minced
- 3 cups spinach
- 2 plum tomatoes, chopped ½ cup mozzarella, shredded
- 2 tbsp. Parmesan cheese, shredded
- 2 tbsp. panko breadcrumbs

Directions:
1.   Preparing the Ingredients.
2.   Heat a Griddle for medium heat.
3.   Grilling
4.   Make sure the grates are clean.
5.   Cheese-Stuffed Sweet Mini Peppers
6.   Maryland Crab Cakes
7.   Eggs in a Basket
8.   Chive Avocado Goat Cheese Omelet

Beets And Greens With Vinaigrette

Servings: 4
Cooking Time: 60 Minutes

Ingredients:
- 1½ pounds small beets, with fresh-looking greens still attached if possible
- ½ cup plus 2 tablespoons good-quality olive oil
- Salt and pepper
- 3 tablespoons fresh lemon juice
- 2 tablespoons minced fresh dill

Directions:
1. Preparing the Ingredients.
2. Heat a Griddle for medium to medium-low direct
3. Grilling
4. Make sure the grates are clean.
5. Cut the greens off the beets. Throw away any wilted or discolored leaves; rinse the remainder well to remove any grit and drain. Trim the root ends of the beets and scrub well under running water. Pat the leaves and beets dry. Toss the beets with 2 tablespoons of the oil and a sprinkle of salt until evenly coated.
6. Place the beets on the grill directly. (No need to wash the bowl.) Cook turning them every 5 to 10 Minutes, until a knife inserted in the center goes through with no resistance, 30 to 40 Minutes total. Transfer to a plate and let sit until cool enough to handle.
7. Toss the beet greens in the reserved bowl to coat in oil. Place the greens on the grill directly. Cook tossing once or twice, until they're bright green and browned in spots, 2 to 5 Minutes total. Keep a close eye on them; if they're on too long, they'll crisp up to the point where they'll shatter. Transfer to a plate.
8. Place the remaining ½ cup oil and the lemon juice in a serving bowl and Beat until thickened. Mix in the dill and some salt and pepper. Peel the skin from the beets and cut into halves or quarters. Cut the stems from the leaves in 1-inch lengths; cut the leaves across into ribbons. Place the beets, leaves, and stems in the bowl and toss with the vinaigrette until coated. Serve warm or at room temperature. Or make up to several hours ahead, cover, and refrigerate to serve chilled.

Corn On The Cob

Servings: 4
Cooking Time: 30 Minutes

Ingredients:
- 4 ears fresh corn
- Salt and pepper
- Butter (optional)

Directions:
1. Preparing the Ingredients.
2. Heat a Griddle for medium heat.
3. Grilling.
4. Make sure the grates are clean.
5. Shuck the corn, removing the husks and silks.
6. Place the corn on the grill directly. Cook turning the ears every few Minutes, until some of the kernels char a bit, 8 to 12 Minutes total. Serve with salt, pepper, and butter if you like.

Orange-glazed Carrots Or Parsnips

Servings: 4
Cooking Time: 50 Minutes

Ingredients:
- 8 tablespoons (1 stick) butter or good-quality olive oil
- 1½ pounds carrots or parsnips, trimmed and peeled
- Salt and pepper
- Grated zest of 1 large orange
- 2 tablespoons fresh orange juice
- Chopped fresh parsley, dill, mint, basil, or chervil leaves for garnish (optional)

Directions:
1. Preparing the Ingredients.
2. Heat a Griddle for medium indirect
3. Grilling.
4. Make sure the grates are clean.
5. Melt the butter in a small saucepan over medium heat. Remove from the heat. Sprinkle with salt and pepper and mix in the orange zest and juice. Brush the carrots with the butter; keep the remaining butter mixture warm.
6. Place the carrots on the grill directly, with the thick ends just over indirect heat. Cook turning them every 5 Minutes or so, until a knife inserted at the thickest part goes in without resistance, 20 to 40 Minutes total. (Cook less if you prefer them more crisp-tender.)

7. Transfer to a cutting board, cut into pieces, and Place in a serving dish. Spry over the remaining flavored butter and toss to coat. Sprinkle with fresh herbs if you're using them and serve.

Crisp Broccoli

Servings: 4
Cooking Time: 30 Minutes
Ingredients:
- 1½ pounds broccoli
- 2 tablespoons good-quality olive oil
- Salt and pepper

Directions:
1. Preparing the Ingredients
2. Heat a Griddle for medium-high heat. Grilling. Make sure the grates are clean.
3. Cut the broccoli into florets or spears, as you like. Place on a baking sheet, pour over the oil, sprinkle with salt and pepper, and toss until the broccoli is evenly coated. If grilling florets, transfer to a perforated grill pan right before you take them out to the grill.
4. Place the broccoli on the grill directly.
5. Grilling
6. Turning often, until crisp tender, 5 to 15 Minutes total, depending on how crunchy or charred you want it. Transfer to a platter, taste and adjust the seasoning, and serve.

Eggplant With Garlic

Servings: 4
Cooking Time: 30 Minutes
Ingredients:
- 2 medium or 1 large eggplant (1½–2 pounds)
- 1 tablespoon minced garlic, or more to taste
- 6 tablespoons good-quality olive oil
- Salt and pepper
- Chopped fresh parsley for garnish

Directions:
1. Preparing the Ingredients.
2. Heat a Griddle for medium-high heat.
3. Grilling.
4. Make sure the grates are clean.

5. Peel the eggplant if you like and cut it across into ½-inch slices. Mix the garlic into the oil along with salt and pepper; brush on the slices on both sides.
6. Place the eggplant slices on the grill directly. Cook turning and basting with the garlic oil, until the slices are browned and fork-tender, 10 to 15 Minutes total. Transfer to a platter, spry with any remaining oil, sprinkle with parsley, and serve hot, warm, or at room temperature. Or transfer to an airtight container and refrigerate for up to a few days.

Bread Pudding With Rosemary

Servings: 4
Cooking Time: 1 Hour
Ingredients:
- 5 tablespoons good-quality olive oil
- 2 pounds cremini mushrooms, trimmed
- Salt and pepper
- 1 large onion, cut into ½-inch wedges
- 1 12-ounce loaf ciabatta bread, split lengthwise
- 3 eggs
- 4 cups milk
- 4 tablespoons (½ stick) butter, melted, plus more for the pan
- 2 tablespoons chopped fresh rosemary
- 2 cups grated Gruyère, Emmental, cheddar, or Jack cheese (about 8 ounces)

Directions:
1. Preparing the Ingredients.
2. If you're using bamboo or wooden skewers, soak them in water for 30 Minutes. Heat a Griddle for medium heat.
3. Grilling
4. Make sure the grates are clean.
5. Place 3 tablespoons of the oil in a large bowl. Add the mushrooms, sprinkle with salt and pepper, and toss until coated. Skewer the mushrooms through their sides. Thread the onion on skewers and brush with the remaining 2 tablespoons oil.
6. Place the skewers on the grill (Place the mushrooms cap down, if possible) directly. Cook until everything softens. The mushrooms will take about 5 Minutes; there is no need to turn them. The onions will take 15 to 25 Minutes; turn them several times. It's fine if they char a bit.

7. When you take the mushrooms off, Place the bread on the grill cut side down, and let brown and crisp, about 5 Minutes, then turn and grill another 3 to 4 Minutes. Transfer the vegetables to a platter and the bread to a cutting board. When cool enough to handle, remove the vegetables from the skewers and cut the bread into 1½-inch cubes. Slice the mushrooms and cut the onions into pieces.

8. Beat the eggs in a large bowl, then Beat in the milk and melted butter. Mix in the rosemary and some salt and pepper, then add the bread, pushing it down into the milk multiple times, if necessary, to make sure all if it gets coated. Let sit for 15 to 20 Minutes at room temperature, pushing down on the bread every few Minutes.

9. Coat a 9- × 13-inch baking pan with butter. Mix the mushrooms and onions into the bread custard, then add the cheese and mix until distributed evenly. Pour into the pan. (You can make the bread pudding to this point up to a day before; cover and refrigerate until you're ready to bake it.)

10. Heat the oven to 350°F. Place the pan on the center rack and bake until a thin knife inserted in the center comes out clean or nearly so, 45 to 60 Minutes, or a bit longer if baking straight from the refrigerator. Serve hot.

Grilled Onions

Servings: 4
Cooking Time: 50 Minutes
Ingredients:
- 1½ pounds onions, peeled
- About 2 tablespoons good-quality olive oil
- Salt and pepper

Directions:

1. Preparing the Ingredients.
2. Heat a Griddle for medium to medium-low heat.
3. Grilling
4. Make sure the grates are clean.
5. Cut the onions through the equator (not root end to stem end) into slices at least 1 inch thick. (If the onions are flat-shaped, simply halve them.) Brush the slices with oil and carefully sprinkle with salt and pepper on both sides.
6. Place the onion slices on the grill directly. Cook turning once, until they brown and are soft all the

way through, 10 to 15 Minutes per side. Check them a few Minutes after you Place them on; if they're coloring too quickly. Transfer to a platter and serve hot, warm, or at room temperature.

Smoked Pork Sausage Hakka Noodles Recipe

Servings: 4 Slices
Cooking Time: 15 Minutes
Ingredients:
- 1 packet Hakka Noodles
- 5 Smoked Pork Sausages
- 50g Coriander Leaves
- 1 tbsp. Soya Sauce
- 50g Mint Leaves
- 1 Onion
- 3 Green Chilies
- 1 Capsicum
- Salt to Taste

Directions:

1. Cut and slice all the pork vegetables and keep it aside.
2. Then cook the packet of Hakka noodle in a container. Make sure to add a little bit of oil so that they don't stick together. Boil the noodles for 5-6 minutes.
3. Take the noodles and transfer them to a strainer and wash them under the tap so that they stop cooking.
4. Then add a little bit of oil and soya sauce to the noodles. Once this is ready, we are ready to cook the rest of the meal.
5. Prepare griddle for medium heat. Lightly oil. Add the onions and chilies till they turn light brown.
6. Then add the smoked pork sausages and cook it for 5 – 7 minutes.
7. Add the coriander and mint leaves and cook for another 5 minutes. The major aroma will be from the coriander and mint leaves.
8. Then add the cauliflower, capsicum and salt to taste.
9. Then add the noodles and then cook it for another 5 minutes.
10. Take it off the griddle and then serve it with mint leaves.

Nutrition Info: (Per serving):Calories 220.2kcal; protein 25.7 g; carbs 33.2 g; fat 23g

Shrimp With Yogurt Sauce

Servings: 4
Cooking Time: 30 Minutes
Ingredients:
- 4 scallions, trimmed and cut into pieces
- 2 cloves garlic, peeled
- 1 small bunch fresh parsley, thick stems removed (thin stems are fine)
- 1 cup yogurt
- Salt and pepper
- 2 pounds large or jumbo shrimp, peeled (and deveined if you like)
- Lemon wedges for serving

Directions:
1. Preparing the Ingredients.
2. Place the scallions, garlic, parsley, and yogurt in a blender or food processor, sprinkle with salt and pepper, and purée until smooth. Transfer to a large bowl, add the shrimp, and toss to coat fully with the marinade. Marinate at room temperature while the grill heats up, or cover and refrigerate for up to several hours.
3. 2 Heat a Griddle for hot direct
4. Grilling
5. Make sure the grates are clean.
6. Place the shrimp on the grill directly. Cook turning once, until the shrimp are opaque all the way through, 3 to 5 Minutes per side, depending on their size and how hot the it is. Discard any remaining marinade. Transfer to a platter and serve with lemon wedges.

Summer Squash With Sea Salt

Servings: 4
Cooking Time: 30 Minutes
Ingredients:
- 1½ pounds summer squash or zucchini
- Good-quality olive oil for brushing
- Salt

Directions:
1. Preparing the Ingredients.
2. Heat a Griddle for medium heat.
3. Grilling.
4. Make sure the grates are clean.
5. Trim the ends from the squash and cut in half lengthwise, or through the equator if using pattypan. Brush with oil on all sides, and sprinkle the cut sides with salt.
6. Place the squash on the grill directly. Cook turning once, until fork-tender, 3 to 5 Minutes per side. Transfer to a platter and serve.

Grilled Kale With Lemon

Servings: 4
Cooking Time: 25 Minutes
Ingredients:
- 1½ pounds lacinato kale
- ¼ cup good-quality olive oil
- Salt and pepper
- ½ lemon, cut into wedges

Directions:
1. Preparing the Ingredients.
2. Heat a Griddle for medium heat.
3. Grilling.
4. Make sure the grates are clean.
5. Cut the stems from the leaves; save them for another use if you like. Rip the leaves into pieces if you like (but not too small). Place the oil in a large bowl. Add the leaves and massage them around until they are completely coated. Sprinkle with salt and pepper, and toss. (You can prepare the kale to this point up to several hours ahead and refrigerate in a plastic zipper bag until you're ready to grill.)
6. Place the leaves on the grill directly; it's okay if they overlap. Cook until the leaves develop some char, 2 to 4 Minutes. Turn and cook, spreading them into a single layer as they shrink, until charred on the other side, another 1 to 3 Minutes. As they finish, immediately transfer to a platter. Serve with the lemon wedges.

Hearts Of Romaine With Marinade Sauce

Servings: 4
Cooking Time: 20 Minutes
Ingredients:

- 3 tablespoons red wine vinegar
- 1 tablespoon Dijon mustard
- Salt and pepper
- ½ cup good-quality olive oil
- 4 hearts of romaine lettuce

Directions:

1. Preparing the Ingredients.
2. Heat a Griddle for medium heat.
3. Grilling
4. Make sure the grates are clean.
5. Place the vinegar and mustard in a large bowl with some salt and pepper and Beat to combine. While still whisking, add the oil in a steady stream; keep whisking until thick.
6. Trim the bottoms of the romaine just enough to remove the tough ends but keep the leaves attached. Remove any damaged outer leaves. Transfer the lettuce to the bowl and coat with the vinaigrette, using your hands to work it into the heads as much as you can without bruising the leaves.
7. Place the romaine on the grill directly. Cook turning once, until softened and darkly colored in places, 2 to 5 Minutes per side, depending on how hot it is. Transfer to a platter and serve warm or at room temperature with more pepper sprinkled on top.

Beef With Buttered Noodles

Servings: 4

Cooking Time: 18 Minutes

Ingredients:

- 6 strips bacon
- 1 cup diced onion
- 1 pound thin cut sirloin tip or eye of round beef (about 8 slices)
- ½ cup yellow mustard
- 8 long thin dill pickle slices, cut into ribbons
- 16 ounces American-style lager
- 16 ounces beef stock
- 4 cups noodles, cooked and cooled
- ½ cup finely chopped fresh parsley, for garnish
- Grilling oil, as needed
- salt and pepper, to taste

Directions:

1. Preparing the Ingredients.
2. Bring the griddle to medium-high heat. Cook the bacon for about 10 Minutes until crisp. Cool, crumble into small bits, and set aside.
3. Sauté the diced onion in the bacon grease for about 5 Minutes, until the onions are translucent. Any browned bits of bacon that you can get to release from the griddle and onto the onions will reward you with additional flavor. Allow the onions to cool.
4. To assemble the roulade, sprinkle both sides of a slice of beef with salt and pepper and lay it on a cutting board. If necessary, square off the sides and ends to make a rectangle. Slather a thin coat of mustard on the beef. Place about 2 tablespoons each of the crumbled bacon and onion along one long edge of the beef slice, taking care to leave a perimeter of ¾ inch free of toppings. Add ribbons of pickles to the top of the onion and bacon mixture.
5. Starting at the covered edge of the beef slice, tightly roll the beef, bacon, onions, and pickles toward the opposite side, into a cigar shape. Take care to keep the roulade tight to keep the ingredients inside. Repeat with remaining beef slices and ingredients.
6. Grilling
7. To cook, bring the griddle grill to about medium-high heat. Add Grilling oil to the grill and when it shimmers, place the roulades directly on the griddle with the seam sides down. You want the seam of the roulade to seal as it sears to keep the ingredients from falling out. Allow the seam side to cook for 3 Minutes, then roll the roulades to brown the rest of the meat for another 2 to 3 Minutes per side or until you get a consistently browned exterior.
8. To braise the roulades, place a skillet directly on the griddle surface. Place all of the roulades inside of the skillet in a single layer. In a large bowl, mix the lager and broth and use 1 to 2 cups as braising liquid, or enough so the meat is about 80 percent covered in liquid. (If you prefer to omit the beer, you can simply double the amount of beef broth.)
9. Cover the skillet and leave a small gap so the steam can escape. Allow the liquid to reduce by about half, 15 to 20 Minutes, then carefully rotate the roulades so the portion that was not in the braising liquid is now covered. Add an additional 1 to 2 cups of liquid and allow it to reduce over medium heat for 15 to 20 Minutes. The meat should be fork tender

with just the right amount of give from your initial searing efforts.

10.   While the liquid is reducing, coat a clean part of your griddle with butter and cook the noodles in the butter. Flip with a large spatula to get some brownness and texture on them.

11.   To serve, place a bed of noodles on each plate with two roulades on top. Any reduced braising liquid can be whimsically spryd on top of the noodles and beef for an additional boost of flavor. Garnish with chopped parsley.

Grill-roasted Plum Tomatoes

Servings: 4
Cooking Time: 3½ Hours
Ingredients:
- 4 plum tomatoes (or as many as you have room for)
- Good-quality olive oil for brushing
- Salt and pepper

Directions:
1.   Preparing the Ingredients.
2.   Heat a Griddle for medium to low indirect
3.   Grilling
4.   Make sure the grates are clean.
5.   Cut the tomatoes in half lengthwise. Brush them with oil and sprinkle the cut sides with salt and pepper.
6.   Place the tomatoes on the indirect side of the grill, cut side up. If the temperture is closer to medium, keep the tomatoes some distance from the heat to avoid charring. Close the grill and cook until shriveled but you can still see signs of moisture, at least 1 hour and up to 3 hours. About halfway through, move and rotate the tomatoes so they cook evenly.
7.   Transfer to a platter and serve hot, warm, or at room temperature. These will keep in an airtight container in the refrigerator for up to a week and in the freezer for several months.

Steak

Servings: 4-5 Slices
Cooking Time: 10 Minutes
Ingredients:
- 1 steak
- 1 salt
- 1 pepper

Directions:
1.   This recipe is for any number of steaks including sirloin, T-bone, ribeye, etc.
2.   Season your steak with salt and pepper, or any other seasoning of your choice.
3.   Prepare griddle for medium-high heat. Lightly oil. Place steak on griddle.
4.   When one side develops a crust, flip once. Until the steak is done to your desired doneness.
5.   The most important point to remember when griddling a steak is to leave it alone. Let the juices, the seasoning and the heat make an excellent steak.

Nutrition Info: (Per serving): Calories: 919kcal, Carbs: 4g, Protein: 61g, Fat: 73g

Scallions With Cilantro And Lime

Servings: 4
Cooking Time: 30 Minutes
Ingredients:
- 2 bunches scallions
- Good-quality olive oil for brushing
- Salt and pepper
- 2 limes, 1 halved, 1 cut into wedges
- Tender fresh cilantro sprigs for garnish

Directions:
1.   Preparing the Ingredients.
2.   Heat a Griddle for medium-high heat.
3.   Grilling
4.   Make sure the grates are clean.
5.   Trim the root ends of the scallions and the ragged ends of the greens; leave as much of the greens on as possible. Brush or rub the scallions with the oil until well coated; sprinkle with salt.
6.   Place the scallions on the grill directly, perpendicular to the grates so they don't fall through. Cook turning once or twice, until deeply colored and tender, 5 to 10 Minutes total, depending on their thickness. Transfer to a platter, sprinkle with pepper, and squeeze the juice of the lime halves over all.

Serve hot, warm, or at room temperature, garnished with the cilantro and lime wedges.

Grill-braised Potatoes

Servings: 4
Cooking Time: 45 Minutes
Ingredients:
- 1½ pounds potatoes, cut into ¼-inch-thick slices
- 3 cloves garlic, sliced
- 2 tablespoons good-quality olive oil
- 1 tablespoon chopped fresh marjoram
- Salt and pepper
- 1 tablespoon vegetable broth or water

Directions:
1. Preparing the Ingredients.
2. Heat a Griddle for medium heat.
3. Grilling
4. Place the potatoes, garlic, oil, marjoram, and salt and pepper to taste in a large bowl and toss to combine. Transfer to the center of a 12-inch piece of heavy-duty foil and pour over the broth. Fold over the foil to cover, and crimp the sides shut; you don't want any steam escaping from the packet.
5. Place the packet on the grill directly. Cook until the potatoes are fork tender, 20 to 30 Minutes.
6. Transfer the packet to a platter; the potatoes will keep hot in it for at least 15 Minutes. Be careful of the steam when you undo the foil; transfer to a dish and serve.

Avocado With Lemon

Servings: 4
Cooking Time: 25 Minutes
Ingredients:
- 2 ripe avocados
- Good-quality olive oil for brushing
- 1 lemon, halved
- Salt and pepper

Directions:
1. Preparing the Ingredients.
2. Heat a Griddle for medium heat.
3. Grilling
4. Make sure the grates are clean.
5. Cut the avocados in half lengthwise. Carefully strike a chef's knife into the pit, then wiggle it a bit to lift and remove it. Insert a spoon underneath the flesh against the skin and run it all the way around to separate the entire half of the avocado. Repeat with the other avocado. Brush with oil, then squeeze one of the lemon halves over them thoroughly on both sides so they don't discolor. Cut the other lemon half into 4 wedges.
6. Place the avocados on the grill directly, cut side down. Cook turning once, until browned in places, 5 to 10 Minutes total. Serve the halved avocados as is, or slice and fan them for a prettier presentation. Sprinkle with salt and pepper and garnish with the lemon wedges.

Easy Roasted Okra With Sea Salt

Servings: 4
Cooking Time: 30 Minutes
Ingredients:
- 1½ pounds okra pods, stem ends trimmed
- 2 tablespoons good-quality olive oil
- 2 teaspoons coarse sea salt

Directions:
1. Preparing the Ingredients.
2. Heat a Griddle for medium heat.
3. Grilling.
4. Make sure the grates are clean.
5. Place the okra in a bowl. Spry with the oil and toss to coat completely. Sprinkle with the salt and toss again.
6. Place the okra on the grill directly. Cook turning them once or twice, until the pods turn bright green and a knife inserted in the thickest part goes through without resistance, 5 to 10 Minutes total. Transfer to a platter and serve hot or at room temperature.

Tomatoes With Basil

Servings: 4
Cooking Time: 80 Minutes
Ingredients:

- 3 or 4 fresh tomatoes (1½ pounds)
- Good-quality olive oil for brushing
- Salt and pepper
- ⅓ cup or more torn or chopped fresh basil leaves
- Freshly grated Parmesan cheese (optional)

Directions:
1. Preparing the Ingredients.
2. Heat a Griddle for medium heat.
3. Grilling
4. Make sure the grates are clean.
5. Core the tomatoes and cut each across into 3 or 4 thick slices. Brush them with oil and sprinkle with salt and pepper on both sides.
6. Place the tomato slices on the grill directly. Cook turning once, until they are soft but not mushy, 3 to 5 Minutes per side. (They should be just on the verge of falling apart; you should be able to barely lift them from the grill with a spatula.) Transfer the slices to a platter, sprinkle with basil and some cheese if you like, and serve hot, warm, or at room temperature.

Honey Paprika Chicken Tenders Recipe

Servings: 4 Slices
Cooking Time: 10 Minutes
Ingredients:
- 1 lb. chicken tenders, sliced into finger-thick slices
- 1/2 cup honey
- 1/3 cup dark soy sauce
- 3 tbsps. olive oil
- 1 tbsp. paprika
- 2 tbsps. curry powder
- Salt and pepper to taste

Directions:
1. Preheat your griddle to medium-high.
2. Slice the chicken into half an inch-thick strips so they will cook faster and absorb more flavor.
3. In a bowl, combine the soy sauce, paprika, curry powder, honey, and olive oil.
4. Dump in the chicken and mix. Season with salt and pepper to taste.
5. Let the mixture stand for 10-15 minutes.
6. Place on griddle to cook half-way through.
7. Remove from flat top and transfer to a roasting pan and spread evenly so that the chicken pieces are just 1 layer.
8. Cover with aluminum foil and place roasting pan back on flat top until fully cooked through. Approximately 10 – 12 minutes.
9. Garnish with spring onion and enjoy!

Nutrition Info: (Per serving): Calories: 619kcal, fat: 13g; Carbs: 39g; Protein: 4g

Green Beans

Servings: 4
Cooking Time: 40 Minutes
Ingredients:
- 3 tablespoons good-quality olive oil
- 4 cloves garlic, or more to taste, thinly sliced
- Salt and pepper
- 1½ pounds green beans, trimmed

Directions:
1. Preparing the Ingredients.
2. Place the oil and garlic in a large skillet over the lowest heat possible.
3. Grilling.
4. Shaking the pan occasionally and adjusting the heat if necessary, until the garlic is sizzling steadily. Keep a close eye on the garlic; it shouldn't color at all, but will puff and become quite fragrant. Remove from the heat, sprinkle with salt and pepper, and let sit at room temperature.
5. Heat a Griddle for hot direct Grilling. Make sure the grates are clean.
6. Place the green beans on the grill directly, perpendicular to the grates if you're not using a grill pan. Cook until charred in places and a knife inserted into the center of a bean goes in without any resistance, 3 to 5 Minutes depending on their thickness.
7. If the oil is no longer warm, while the beans are on the grill, Place the skillet back over low to medium heat. Warm the oil just until the garlic starts to sizzle again, then remove from the heat. Transfer the beans directly to the skillet, toss to coat well, taste and adjust the seasoning, and serve.

Grill-steamed Leeks

Servings: 4

Cooking Time: 30 Minutes

Ingredients:

- 4 leeks (1–1½ pounds)
- Salt and pepper
- Good-quality olive oil

Directions:

1. Preparing the Ingredients.
2. Heat a Griddle for medium to medium-low heat.
3. Grilling.
4. Make sure the grates are clean.
5. Trim the root ends of the leeks and cut away the tough green tops. Make a long vertical slit through the center of the leek from the root end through the remaining green part, but not cutting all the way through to the other side. Rinse well to get the sand out from between the layers. Sprinkle both sides with salt.
6. Open up the leeks and Place them on the grill directly, cut side down, pressing down gently with a spatula to make sure the layers fan out over the heat. Cook until they have fully softened, 6 to 8 Minutes, depending on their thickness. Brush with some oil, turn, and cook until the bottom browns, 1 to 3 Minutes. Brush the top with oil, turn, and cook another 1 to 3 Minutes. Transfer the leeks to a plate, sprinkle with pepper, and serve hot, warm, or at room temperature.

POULTRY RECIPES

Caesar Marinated Grilled Chicken

Servings: 3
Cooking Time: 24 Minutes
Ingredients:

* ¼ cup crouton
* 1 teaspoon lemon zest. Form into ovals, skewer and grill.
* 1/2 cup Parmesan
* 1/4 cup breadcrumbs
* 1-pound ground chicken
* 2 tablespoons Caesar dressing and more for drizzling
* 2-4 romaine leaves

Directions:

1. Preparing the Ingredients. In a shallow dish, mix well chicken, 2 tablespoons Caesar dressing, parmesan, and breadcrumbs. Mix well with hands. Form into 1-inch oval patties.
2. Thread chicken pieces in skewers. Bring the griddle grill to high heat. When the griddle is hot, put the skewers and cook for 12 Minutes. Halfway through cooking time, turnover skewers. Serve and enjoy on a bed of lettuce and sprinkle with croutons and extra dressing.

Nutrition Info: (Per Serving): CALORIES: 339; FAT: 18.9G; PROTEIN:32.6G; SUGAR:1G

California Seared Chicken

Servings: 4
Cooking Time: 20 Minutes
Ingredients:

* 4 boneless, skinless chicken breasts
* 3/4 cup balsamic vinegar
* 2 tablespoons extra virgin olive oil
* 1 tablespoon honey
* 1 teaspoon oregano
* 1 teaspoon basil
* 1 teaspoon garlic powder
* For garnish:
* Sea salt
* Black pepper, fresh ground
* 4 slices fresh mozzarella cheese
* 4 slices avocado
* 4 slices beefsteak tomato
* Balsamic glaze, for drizzling

Directions:

1. Whisk together balsamic vinegar, honey, olive oil, oregano, basil and garlic powder in a large mixing bowl.
2. Add chicken to coat and marinate for 30 minutes in the refrigerator.
3. Preheat griddle to medium-high. Sear chicken for 7 minutes per side, or until a meat thermometer reaches 165°F.
4. Top each chicken breast with mozzarella, avocado, and tomato and tent with foil on the griddle to melt for 2 minutes.
5. Garnish with a drizzle of balsamic glaze, and a pinch of sea salt and black pepper.

Nutrition Info: Calories: 883, Sodium: 449 mg, Dietary Fiber: 15.2 g, Fat: 62.1 g, Carbs: 29.8 g, Protein: 55.3 g.

Hawaiian Chicken

Servings: 5
Cooking Time: 10 Minutes
Ingredients:

* 8 slices Italian bread
* 8 fresh basil leaves
* 8 thinly sliced tomatoes
* 16 slices of Black Pepper Turkey Breast
* 4 pieces of mozzarella cheese
* 4 tbsps. mayonnaise
* Olive oil

Directions:

1. Add chicken into the large zip-lock bag. Mix together ginger, garlic, brown sugar, pineapple juice, and soy sauce and pour over chicken.
2. Seal zip-lock bag shake well and place in the refrigerator overnight.
3. Heat griddle grill to a medium heat.
4. Remove chicken from the zip-lock bag and set aside. Pour marinade in a medium saucepan and simmer for 5-10 minutes.
5. Place chicken on the hot grill and brush with the hot marinade and grill until chicken is cooked or

until the internal temperature of the chicken reaches 165 F. Serve.

Nutrition Info: (Per serving):Calories 523, Carbs 53g, Fat 23g, Protein 27g

Honey Balsamic Marinated Chicken

Servings: 4
Cooking Time: 20 Minutes
Ingredients:

- 2 lbs. boneless, skinless chicken thighs
- 1 teaspoon olive oil
- 1/2 teaspoon sea salt
- 1/4 teaspoon black pepper
- 1/2 teaspoon paprika
- 3/4 teaspoon onion powder
- For the Marinade:
- 2 tablespoons honey
- 2 tablespoons balsamic vinegar
- 2 tablespoons tomato paste
- 1 teaspoon garlic, minced

Directions:

1. Add chicken, olive oil, salt, black pepper, paprika, and onion powder to a sealable plastic bag. Seal and toss to coat, covering chicken with spices and oil; set aside.
2. Whisk together balsamic vinegar, tomato paste, garlic, and honey.
3. Divide the marinade in half. Add one half to the bag of chicken and store the other half in a sealed container in the refrigerator.
4. Seal the bag and toss chicken to coat. Refrigerate for 30 minutes to 4 hours.
5. Preheat a griddle to medium-high.
6. Discard bag and marinade. Add chicken to the griddle and cook 7 minutes per side or until juices run clear and a meat thermometer reads 165°F.
7. During last minute of cooking, brush remaining marinade on top of the chicken thighs.
8. Serve immediately.

Nutrition Info: Calories: 485, Sodium: 438 mg, Dietary Fiber: 0.5 g, Fat: 18.1 g, Carbs: 11 g, Protein: 66.1 g.

Chicken Breasts Grilled With Feta And Fresh Mint

Servings: 4
Cooking Time: 14 Minutes
Ingredients:

- 2 whole skinless, boneless chicken breasts
- 1piece (1½ ounces) feta cheese, thinly
- sliced
- 8 fresh mint leaves, rinsed, blotted dry,
- and cut into thin slivers
- Coarse salt (kosher or sea)
- Freshly ground black pepper
- 1 tablespoon fresh lemon juice
- 1 tablespoon extra-virgin olive oil
- Lemon wedges, for serving
- YOU'LL ALSO NEED:
- Wooden toothpicks

Directions:

1. Preparing the Ingredients.
2. If using whole chicken breasts, cut each in half. Trim any sinews or excess fat off the chicken breasts and discard. Remove the tenders from the chicken breasts and set them aside. Place a half breast at the edge of a cutting board. Cut a deep horizontal pocket in the breast, taking care not to pierce the edges. Repeat with the remaining breast halves. Place 2 or 3 slices of feta and a few slivers of mint in the pocket of each chicken breast. Pin the pockets shut with lightly oiled toothpicks. Place the breasts in a baking dish just large enough to hold them. Season the breasts on both sides with salt and pepper and sprinkle any remaining mint over them. Drizzle the lemon juice and olive oil over both sides of the chicken breasts, patting them onto the meat with your fingers. Let the chicken breasts marinate in the refrigerator, covered, for 20 Minutes, turning once or twice.
3. Turn control knob to the high position, when the griddle is hot, place the chicken breasts on the griddle and cook for 10 to 14 Minutes. Insert an instant-read meat thermometer into the thick part of a breast through one end: The internal temperature should be about 160°F.
4. Transfer the chicken breasts to a platter or plates and remove and discard the toothpicks. Serve the chicken at once with lemon wedges.

Lemony Chicken Paillards With Asparagus And Feta

Servings: 4
Cooking Time: 6 Minutes
Ingredients:
- 1 pound thin asparagus
- 1 tablespoon good-quality olive oil, plus more for brushing
- Salt and pepper
- 1½ pounds boneless, skinless chicken breasts, cut and pounded into paillards
- ½ cup crumbled feta cheese
- Lemon wedges for serving

Directions:
1. Preparing the Ingredients
2. Cut off the bottoms of the asparagus, then toss the spears with 1 tablespoon oil and sprinkle with salt. Put them on the griddle grill and cook, turning once, until browned and crisp-tender, 3 to 5 Minutes. Transfer to a plate.
3. Brush the paillards with oil and sprinkle with salt and pepper on both sides. Put them on the griddle grill and cook, turning once, until the chicken is no longer pink in the center, 2 to 3 Minutes per side. (Nick with a small knife and peek inside.) Transfer to individual plates, top with the asparagus, sprinkle with feta, and serve with the lemon wedges.

Hawaiian Chicken Skewers

Servings: 4 - 5
Cooking Time: 15 Minutes
Ingredients:
- 1 lb. boneless, skinless chicken breast, cut into 1 ½ inch cubes
- 3 cups pineapple, cut into 1 ½ inch cubes
- 2 large green peppers, cut into 1 ½ inch pieces
- 1 large red onion, cut into 1 ½ inch pieces
- 2 tablespoons olive oil, to coat veggies
- For the marinade:
- 1/3 cup tomato paste
- 1/3 cup brown sugar, packed
- 1/3 cup soy sauce
- 1/4 cup pineapple juice
- 2 tablespoons olive oil
- 1 1/2 tablespoon mirin or rice wine vinegar
- 4 teaspoons garlic cloves, minced
- 1 tablespoon ginger, minced
- 1/2 teaspoon sesame oil
- Pinch of sea salt
- Pinch of ground black pepper
- 10 wooden skewers, for assembly

Directions:
1. Combine marinade ingredients in a mixing bowl until smooth. Reserve a 1/2 cup of the marinade in the refrigerator.
2. Add chicken and remaining marinade to a sealable plastic bag and refrigerate for 1 hour.
3. Soak 10 wooden skewer sticks in water for 1 hour.
4. Preheat the griddle to medium heat.
5. Add red onion, bell pepper and pineapple to a mixing bowl with 2 tablespoons olive oil and toss to coat.
6. Thread red onion, bell pepper, pineapple and chicken onto the skewers until all of the chicken has been used.
7. Place skewers on griddle and grab your reserved marinade from the refrigerator; cook for 5 minutes then brush with remaining marinade and rotate.
8. Brush again with marinade and sear about 5 additional minutes or until chicken reads 165°F on a meat thermometer.
9. Serve warm.

Nutrition Info: Calories: 311, Sodium: 1116 mg, Dietary Fiber: 4.2 g, Fat: 8.8 g, Carbs: 38.1 g, Protein: 22.8g.

Double-stuffed Bone-in Chicken Breasts

Servings: 4
Cooking Time: 20 Minutes
Ingredients:
- 1 lemon
- 6 tablespoons (¾ stick) butter, softened
- 1–2 tablespoons any chopped fresh herb
- Salt and pepper
- 3 bone-in, skin-on chicken breast halves (1¾ to 2 pounds total)

Directions:
1. Preparing the Ingredients

2.   1 Finely grate the zest of the lemon, then cut the lemon into thin slices. Mash the butter, zest, and herb together in a small bowl with some salt and pepper. Taste and adjust the seasoning.

3.   Working with the skin side up, cut a slit into the thickest part of the breast with the tip of a small sharp knife. Keeping the opening slit just large enough for your finger (this will help the filling stay in the pocket), work the knife back and forth to create as big a pocket as possible inside the breast; be careful not to cut through to the other side. Divide the compound butter evenly between the breasts, pushing it into the slit and massaging it to fill the pocket.

4.   Still using your fingers, separate the skin from the meat on one edge so you can work 2 lemon slices underneath to cover as much of the breast as possible. Sprinkle the breasts with salt and pepper and refrigerate. (You can make these to this point up to several hours ahead.)

5.   2 Bring the griddle grill to high heat, when the griddle is hot, put the chicken skin side up and cook until firm when pressed and browned on top, 15 to 20 Minutes. Turn to crisp the skin; cook for another 5 Minutes. If the chicken is still pink at the bone at the thickest point, turn skin side up again to finish cooking. (Nick with a small knife and peek inside.) Transfer the chicken to a platter and let rest for 5 Minutes.

Chicken Fried Rice

Servings: 4
Cooking Time: 20 Minutes
Ingredients:
- 2 boneless, skinless chicken breasts, cut into small pieces
- 4 cups long grain rice, cooked and allowed to air dry
- 1/3 cup soy sauce
- 1 yellow onion, finely chopped
- 4 cloves garlic, finely chopped
- 1 cups petite peas
- 2 carrots sliced into thin rounds
- 1/2 cup corn kernels
- 1/4 cup vegetable oil
- 2 tablespoons butter

Directions:
1.   Preheat griddle to medium-high.
2.   Add the vegetable oil to the griddle.
3.   When the oil is shimmering, add the onion, carrot, peas, and corn.
4.   Cook for several minutes, until lightly charred.
5.   Add the chicken and cook until just browned.
6.   Add the rice, soy sauce, garlic, and butter.
7.   Toss until the rice is tender and the vegetables are just softened.
8.   Serve immediately.
Nutrition Info: Calories: 485, Sodium: 1527 mg, Dietary Fiber: 4.7g, Fat: 20.8g, Carbs: 60.9g Protein: 13.4g

Hasselback Stuffed Chicken

Servings: 4
Cooking Time: 30 Minutes
Ingredients:
- 4 boneless, skinless chicken breasts
- 2 tablespoons olive oil
- 2 tablespoons taco seasoning
- 1/2 red, yellow and green pepper, very thinly sliced
- 1 small red onion, very thinly sliced
- 1/2 cup Mexican shredded cheese
- Guacamole, for serving
- Sour cream, for serving
- Salsa, for serving

Directions:
1.   Preheat griddle to med-high.
2.   Cut thin horizontal cuts across each chicken breast; like you would hasselback potatoes.
3.   Rub chicken evenly with olive oil and taco seasoning.
4.   Add a mixture of bell peppers and red onions to each cut, and place the breasts on the griddle.
5.   Cook chicken for 15 minutes.
6.   Remove and top with cheese.
7.   Tent loosely with foil and cook another 5 minutes, until cheese is melted.
8.   Remove from griddle and top with guacamole, sour cream and salsa. Serve alongside your favorite side dishes!

Nutrition Info: Calories:643 , Sodium:1549 mg, Dietary Fiber: 3.8 g, Fat: 18.6g, Carbs: 26.3g, Protein: 93.3g.

Chicken Satay With Thai Peanut Sauce

Servings: 4
Cooking Time: 8 Minutes
Ingredients:
* 3 large boneless skinless chicken breasts or 6 boneless skinless thighs
* satay sticks
* THAI PEANUT SAUCE
* 1 cup creamy peanut butter
* ¾ cup coconut milk
* 3 Tbsp. soy sauce
* 3 Tbsp. fresh lime juice
* 3 Tbsp. brown sugar
* 2 Tbsp. sesame oil
* 2 tsp. crushed red pepper flakes
* 1 Tbsp. fish sauce
* 1 Tbsp. sriracha sauce
* 1 (3-in.) piece of ginger, peeled and diced
* 2 cloves garlic, minced
* ¼ cup chopped cilantro

Directions:
1. Preparing the Ingredients
2. Cut chicken into 1.5-inch squares and place onto satay sticks. Lightly season with salt. Combine all ingredients for sauce except the cilantro into a saucepan. Place saucepan over medium heat, mix ingredients together using a whisk, and let simmer for 5 Minutes. Once ingredients have melded together, use either a blender or an immersion blender to blend until smooth. Pour into bowl and top with cilantro.
3. Turn control knob to the high position, when the griddle is hot, place the chicken breasts and cook for 8 Minutes. Because the chicken is cut into small pieces, it will cook rather quick. But don't risk undercooked chicken. Ensure internal temperature meets minimum requirements of 165° Fahrenheit. Remove from grill.
4. Serve with sauce and cilantro.

Greek Chicken

Servings: 2
Cooking Time: 15 Minutes
Ingredients:
* 2 chicken breasts, skinless and boneless
* 2 tbsp olive oil
* 1 tsp Italian seasoning
* 1 1/2 cup grape tomatoes, cut in half
* 1/2 cup olives
* 1/4 tsp pepper
* 1/4 tsp salt

Directions:
1. Season chicken with Italian seasoning, pepper, and salt.
2. Preheat the griddle to medium-low heat. Add oil to the griddle top.
3. Add season chicken onto the hot griddle top and cook for 4-6 minutes on each side. Transfer chicken on a plate.
4. Add tomatoes and olives onto the griddle top cook for 2-4 minutes.
5. Pour olive and tomato mixture on top of the chicken and serve.

Nutrition Info: (Per Serving): Calories 468 ;Fat 29.4 g ;Carbohydrates 7.8 g ;Sugar 3.8 g ;Protein 43.8 g ;Cholesterol 132 mg

Tarragon Chicken Tenders

Servings: 4
Cooking Time: 5 Minutes
Ingredients:
* FOR THE CHICKEN:
* 1½ pounds chicken tenders (12 to 16
* tenders)
* Coarse salt (kosher or sea) and freshly
* ground black pepper
* 3 tablespoons chopped fresh tarragon
* leaves, plus 4 whole sprigs for garnish
* 1 teaspoon finely grated lemon zest
* 2 tablespoons fresh lemon juice
* 2 tablespoons extra-virgin olive oil
* FOR THE SAUCE (OPTIONAL):
* 2 tablespoons fresh lemon juice
* 2 tablespoons salted butter

- ½ cup heavy (whipping) cream

Directions:

1. Preparing the Ingredients
2. Make the chicken: Place the chicken tenders in a nonreactive baking dish just large enough to hold them in a single layer. Season the tenders generously on both sides with salt and pepper. Sprinkle the chopped tarragon and lemon zest all over the tenders, patting them onto the chicken with your fingertips. Drizzle the lemon juice and the olive oil over the tenders and pat them onto the chicken. Let the tenders marinate in the refrigerator, covered, for 10 Minutes.
3. Drain the chicken tenders well by lifting one end with tongs and letting the marinade drip off. Discard the marinade.
4. Bring the griddle grill to high heat. When the griddle is hot, place the chicken tenders on the griddle. The chicken tenders will be done after cooking 3 to 5 Minutes. Use the poke test to check for doneness; the chicken should feel firm when pressed.
5. Transfer the chicken tenders to a platter or plates. If making the sauce, place the lemon juice and the butter in a small saucepan or in the grill pan over medium heat. Add the cream and bring to a boil (use a wooden spoon to scrape up the brown bits from between the ridges of the grill pan). Let the sauce boil until thickened, 3 to 5 Minutes. Pour the lemon cream sauce over the chicken tenders and serve at once.

Chicken Thighs With Ginger-sesame Glaze

Servings: 4 - 8
Cooking Time: 20 Minutes
Ingredients:
- 8 boneless, skinless chicken thighs
- For the glaze:
- 3 tablespoons dark brown sugar
- 2 1/2 tablespoons soy sauce
- 1 tablespoon fresh garlic, minced
- 2 teaspoons sesame seeds
- 1 teaspoon fresh ginger, minced
- 1 teaspoon sambal oelek
- 1/3 cup scallions, thinly sliced
- Non-stick cooking spray

Directions:

1. Combine glaze ingredients in a large mixing bowl; separate and reserve half for serving.
2. Add chicken to bowl and toss to coat well.
3. Preheat the griddle to medium-high heat.
4. Coat with cooking spray.
5. Cook chicken for 6 minutes on each side or until done.
6. Transfer chicken to plates and drizzle with remaining glaze to serve.
Nutrition Info: Calories: 301, Sodium: 413 mg, Dietary Fiber: 0.3 g, Fat: 11.2g, Carbs: 4.7g, Protein: 42.9g.

Chicken Satay With Almond Butter Sauce

Servings: 4
Cooking Time: 8 Minutes
Ingredients:
- 1 lb. boneless, skinless chicken thighs, cut into thin strips
- Olive oil, for brushing
- For the marinade:
- 1/2 cup canned light coconut milk
- 1/2 lime, juiced
- 1 tablespoon honey
- 2 teaspoons soy sauce
- 1 1/2 teaspoons fish sauce
- 1/2 teaspoon red chili flakes
- 2 teaspoons ginger, grated
- 1 clove of garlic, grated
- 1/2 teaspoon curry powder
- 1/4 teaspoon ground coriander
- For the almond butter sauce:
- 1/4 cup almond butter
- 1/4 cup water
- 2 tablespoons canned, light coconut milk
- 1 tablespoon honey
- 1/2 lime, juiced
- 1 teaspoon fish sauce
- 1 teaspoon fresh grated ginger
- 1/2 teaspoon low sodium soy sauce
- 1/2 teaspoon Sriracha

Directions:

1. Whisk together all of the ingredients for the marinade in a medium mixing bowl.

2. Add chicken to mixing bowl and toss to coat.
3. Cover and refrigerate 2 hours or overnight.
4. Preheat griddle to medium high heat and brush with olive oil.
5. Thread the chicken strips onto metal skewers.
6. Place the chicken skewers on the prepared griddle and cook 3 minutes, rotate, and cook another 4 minutes or until the chicken is cooked through.
7. Whisk together all of the ingredients for the almond butter sauce in a small saucepan.
8. Bring the sauce to a boil on medium heat, then lower to medium low and simmer for 1 to 2 minutes or until the sauce thickens.
9. Serve chicken satay warm with the almond butter sauce and enjoy.
Nutrition Info: Calories: 347, Sodium: 743 mg, Dietary Fiber: 1.2g, Fat: 19.7g, Carbs: 8.6g, Protein: 34.3g.

Honey Sriracha Grilled Chicken Thighs

Servings: 6
Cooking Time: 35 Minutes
Ingredients:
- 2.5 lbs. boneless chicken thighs
- 3 tablespoons butter, unsalted
- 1 tablespoon fresh ginger, minced
- 2 garlic cloves, minced
- 1/4 teaspoon smoked paprika
- 1/4 teaspoon chili powder
- 4 tablespoons honey
- 3 tablespoons Sriracha
- 1 tablespoon lime juice

Directions:
1. Preheat griddle to medium high.
2. Melt butter in a small saucepan on medium low heat; when melted add ginger and garlic. Stir until fragrant, about 2 minutes.
3. Fold in smoked paprika, ground cloves, honey, Sriracha and lime juice. Stir to combine, turn heat to medium and simmer for 5 minutes.
4. Rinse and pat chicken thighs dry.
5. Season with salt and pepper on both sides.
6. Spray griddle with non-stick cooking spray.

7. Place chicken thighs on grill, skin side down first. Grill for 5 minutes. Flip the chicken over and grill on the other side for 5 minutes.
8. Continue to cook chicken, flipping every 3 minutes, so it doesn't burn, until the internal temperature reads 165ºF on a meat thermometer.
9. During the last 5 minutes of grilling brush the glaze on both sides of the chicken.
10. Remove from grill and serve warm.
Nutrition Info: Calories: 375, Sodium: 221 mg, Dietary Fiber: 0.3g, Fat: 22.5g, Carbs: 14.7g Protein: 32g

Chicken & Broccoli Stir Fry

Servings: 4
Cooking Time: 15 Minutes
Ingredients:
- 1 lb chicken breast, skinless, boneless, and cut into chunks
- 1 tbsp soy sauce
- 1 tbsp ginger, minced
- 1/2 tsp garlic powder
- 1 tbsp olive oil
- 1/2 onion, sliced
- 2 cups broccoli florets
- 2 tsp hot sauce
- 2 tsp vinegar
- 1 tsp sesame oil
- Pepper
- Salt

Directions:
1. Add all ingredients into the large mixing bowl and toss well.
2. Preheat the griddle to medium heat.
3. Spray griddle top with cooking spray.
4. Transfer chicken and broccoli mixture onto the hot griddle top and cook until broccoli is tender and chicken is cooked.
5. Serve and enjoy.
Nutrition Info: (Per Serving): Calories 200 ;Fat 7 g ;Carbohydrates 6 g ;Sugar 1.6 g ;Protein 26 g ;Cholesterol 73 mg

Fiery Italian Chicken Skewers

Servings: 2 -4
Cooking Time: 20 Minutes
Ingredients:
- 10 boneless, skinless chicken thighs, cut into chunks
- 1 large red onion, cut into wedges
- 1 large red pepper, stemmed, seeded, and cut into chunks
- For the marinade:
- 1/3 cup toasted pine nuts
- 1 1/2 cups sliced roasted red peppers
- 5 hot cherry peppers, stemmed and seeded, or to taste
- 1 cup packed fresh basil leaves, plus more to serve
- 4 cloves garlic, peeled
- 1/4 cup grated Parmesan cheese
- 1 tablespoon paprika
- extra virgin olive oil, as needed

Directions:
1. Combine the toasted pine nuts, roasted red peppers, hot cherry peppers, basil, garlic, Parmesan, and paprika in a food processor or blender and process until well-combined.
2. Add in olive oil until the pesto reaches a thin consistency in order to coat the chicken as a marinade.
3. Transfer half of the pesto to a large sealable plastic bag, and reserve the other half for serving.
4. Add the chicken thigh chunks to the bag of pesto, seal, and massage the bag to coat the chicken.
5. Refrigerate for 1 hour.
6. Preheat griddle to medium-high heat and brush with olive oil.
7. Thread the chicken cubes, red onion, and red pepper onto metal skewers.
8. Brush the chicken with the reserved pesto.
9. Cook until the chicken reaches an internal temperature of 165°F; about 5 minutes per side. Serve warm with your favorite salad or vegetables!

Nutrition Info: Calories: 945, Sodium: 798 mg, Dietary Fiber: 3.2 g, Fat: 46.7 g, Carbs: 14.7g, Protein: 112.2g.

Chicken Roast With Pineapple Salsa

Servings: 2
Cooking Time: 45 Minutes
Ingredients:
- ¼ cup extra virgin olive oil
- ¼ cup freshly chopped cilantro
- 1 avocado, diced
- 1-pound boneless chicken breasts
- 2 cups canned pineapples
- 2 teaspoons honey
- Juice from 1 lime
- Salt and pepper to taste

Directions:
1. Preparing the Ingredients.
2. 1 Season the chicken breasts with lime juice, olive oil, honey, salt, and pepper.
3. 2 Bring the griddle grill to high heat. When the griddle is hot, place on the griddle and cook for 45 Minutes.
4. Flip the chicken every 10 Minutes to grill all sides evenly.
5. Once the chicken is cooked, serve with pineapples, cilantro, and avocado.

Nutrition Info: (Per Serving): CALORIES: 744; FAT: 32.8G; PROTEIN:4.7G; SUGAR:5G

Sweet Thai Cilantro Chili Chicken Quarters

Servings: 5
Cooking Time: 5 Minutes
Ingredients:
- 4 chicken leg quarters, lightly coated with olive oil
- 1 cup and 1 tsp. water
- ¾ cup rice vinegar
- ½ cup white sugar
- 3 Tbsp. freshly chopped cilantro
- 2 Tbsp. freshly minced ginger root
- 2 tsp. freshly minced garlic
- 2 Tbsp. crushed red pepper flakes
- 2 Tbsp. ketchup
- 2 Tbsp. cornstarch
- 2 Tbsp. fresh basil chiffonade ("chiffonade" is fancy for "thinly sliced")

Directions:
1. Preparing the Ingredients

2. 1 In a medium-sized saucepan, bring 1 cup water and the vinegar to a boil over high heat.

3. Stir in sugar, cilantro, ginger, garlic, red pepper flakes, and ketchup; simmer for 5 Minutes.

4. In small mixing bowl, mix together 1 teaspoon warm water and 2 tablespoons cornstarch. Use a fork for mixing this, and what you'll end up with will resemble white school glue.

5. Slowly whisk the cornstarch mixture into the simmering sauce, and continue mixing until sauce thickens. Set aside.

6. 2 Bring the griddle grill to high heat. When the griddle is hot, place the chicken quarters skin side down and cook for 8 Minutes.

7. At 155°F internal temperature, glaze chicken with sauce and allow to finish cooking to an internal temperature of 165°F. Plate, garnish with basil, and serve.

Chicken Salad With Mango And Fresh Herbs

Servings: 4
Cooking Time: 8 Minutes
Ingredients:
- 1½ pounds boneless, skinless chicken breasts
- ¼ cup olive oil, plus more for brushing
- Salt and pepper
- Grated zest of 1 lime
- 2 tablespoons fresh lime juice
- 1 head Boston lettuce, torn into pieces
- ½ cup whole fresh mint leaves
- 1 ripe mango, peeled, pitted, and cut into 1-inch pieces

Directions:
1. Preparing the Ingredients
2. 1 Brush with oil and sprinkle with salt and pepper on both sides.
3. Turn control knob to the high position, when the griddle is hot, place the chicken on the griddle grill and cook for 8 Minutes. Transfer the chicken to a plate and let rest while you put the rest of the salad together.
4. 2 Make the dressing: Put the ¼ cup oil in a small bowl with the lime zest and juice and a pinch of salt.

Whisk until the dressing thickens; taste and adjust the seasoning.

5. Put the lettuce and mint in a salad bowl and toss to mix. Cut the chicken across the grain into ½-inch slices and put over the greens. Top with the mango pieces, then drizzle with the dressing and serve (or toss before serving if you like).

Honey-mustard Chicken Tenders

Servings: 4
Cooking Time: 3 Minutes
Ingredients:
- ½ cup Dijon mustard
- 2 tablespoons honey
- 2 tablespoons olive oil
- 1 teaspoon freshly ground black pepper
- 2 pounds chicken tenders
- ½ cup walnuts

Directions:
1. Preparing the Ingredients
2. Whisk together the mustard, honey, olive oil, and pepper in a medium bowl. Add the chicken and toss to coat.
3. Finely grind the walnuts by pulsing them in a food processor or putting them in a heavy-duty plastic bag and pounding them with a rolling pin or heavy skillet.
4. Toss the chicken tenders in the ground walnuts to coat them lightly.
5. Bring the griddle grill to high heat. When the griddle is hot, grill the chicken tenders for about 3 Minutes, until they have taken on grill marks and are cooked through. Serve hot, at room temperature, or refrigerate and serve cold.

Nutrition Info: (Per Serving): CALORIES: 444; FAT: 20G; PROTEIN:5G

Sizzling Chicken Fajitas

Servings: 4
Cooking Time: 25 Minutes
Ingredients:
- 4 boneless chicken breast halves, thinly sliced
- 1 yellow onion, sliced
- 1 large green bell pepper, sliced

- 1 large red bell pepper, sliced
- 1 teaspoon ground cumin
- 1 teaspoon garlic powder
- 1 teaspoon onion powder
- 2 tablespoons lime juice
- 1 tablespoon olive oil
- 1/2 teaspoon black pepper
- 1 teaspoon salt
- 3 tablespoons vegetable oil
- 10 flour tortillas

Directions:

1. In a zipperlock bag, combine the chicken, cumin, garlic, onion, lime juice, salt, pepper, and olive oil. Allow to marinate for 30 minutes.
2. Preheat griddle to medium heat.
3. On one side of the griddle add the olive oil and heat until shimmering. Add the onion and pepper and cook until slightly softened.
4. On the other side of the griddle add the marinated chicken and cook until lightly browned.
5. Once chicken is lightly browned, toss together with the onion and pepper and cook until chicken registers 165°F.
6. Remove chicken and vegetables from the griddle and serve with warm tortillas.

Nutrition Info: Calories: 408, Sodium:664 mg, Dietary Fiber: 5.5 g, Fat: 18.3g, Carbs:37.1g, Protein: 25.9g.

Grilled Chicken With Salsa Criolla

Servings: 5
Cooking Time: 6 Minutes
Ingredients:
- 8 chicken thighs, with skin and bones (about 2 pounds total)
- 1 tablespoon extra-virgin olive oil
- Coarse salt (kosher or sea) and freshly ground or cracked black peppercorns
- About 1 tablespoon dried oregano
- SALSA CRIOLLA
- 1 luscious ripe red tomato, seeded (but not peeled) and cut into ¼-inch dice
- 1 small or ½ large red bell pepper, seeded and cut into ¼-inch dice
- 1 small or ½ medium-size onion, cut into ¼-inch dice
- 1 tablespoon finely chopped fresh flat-leaf parsley
- ¼ cup extra-virgin olive oil
- 2 tablespoons red wine vinegar
- Coarse salt (kosher or sea) and freshly ground black pepper

Directions:

1. Preparing the Ingredients
2. Rinse the thighs under cold running water, then drain and blot dry with paper towels. Place a thigh on a work surface skin side down. Using a sharp paring knife, cut along the length of the thigh bone. Cut the meat away from one end of the bone, then pull or scrape the meat from the bone. Cut the meat away from the other end of the bone. Repeat with the remaining thighs. Discard the bones or set them aside for making stock or another use.
3. Lightly brush the chicken thighs all over with olive oil, then season them generously with salt, pepper, and oregano.
4. Bring the griddle grill to high heat. When the griddle is hot, place the chicken thighs on the griddle, and cook for 6 Minutes.
5. Use the poke test to check for doneness; the chicken should feel firm when pressed.
6. Place the tomato, bell pepper, onion, parsley, olive oil, and vinegar in an attractive nonreactive serving bowl and toss to mix. Season with salt and pepper to taste. The sauce can be made several hours ahead.
7. Transfer the chicken thighs to a platter or plates and serve at once with the Salsa Criolla on top or on the side.

Classic Bbq Chicken

Servings: 4-6
Cooking Time: 1 Hour 45 Minutes
Ingredients:
- 4 pounds of your favorite chicken, including legs, thighs, wings, and breasts, skin-on
- Salt
- Olive oil

- 1 cup barbecue sauce, like Hickory Mesquite or homemade

Directions:

1. Rub the chicken with olive oil and salt.
2. Preheat the griddle to high heat.
3. Sear chicken skin side down on the grill for 5-10 minutes.
4. Turn the griddle down to medium low heat, tent with foil and cook for 30 minutes.
5. Turn chicken and baste with barbecue sauce.
6. Cover the chicken again and allow to cook for another 20 minutes.
7. Baste, cover and cook again for 30 minutes; repeat basting and turning during this time.
8. The chicken is done when the internal temperature of the chicken pieces are 165°F and juices run clear.
9. Baste with more barbecue sauce to serve!

Nutrition Info: Calories: 539, Sodium: 684 mg, Dietary Fiber: 0.3 g, Fat: 11.6 g, Carbs: 15.1 g, Protein: 87.6 g.

Chicken Bbq With Sweet And Sour Sauce

Servings: 6
Cooking Time: 40 Minutes
Ingredients:

- ¼ cup minced garlic
- ¼ cup tomato paste
- ¾ cup minced onion
- ¾ cup sugar
- 1 cup soy sauce
- 1 cup water
- 1 cup white vinegar
- 6 chicken drumsticks
- Salt and pepper to taste

Directions:

1. 1 Preparing the Ingredients. Place all Ingredients in a Ziploc bag
2. Allow to marinate for at least 2 hours in the fridge.
3. 2 Bring the griddle grill to high heat. When the griddle is hot, grill the chicken for 40 Minutes.
4. Flip the chicken every 10 Minutes for even grilling.

5. Meanwhile, pour the marinade in a saucepan and heat over medium flame until the sauce thickens.
6. Before serving the chicken, brush with the glaze.

Nutrition Info: (Per Serving): CALORIES: 4607; FAT: 19.7G; PROTEIN:27.8G; SUGAR:3G

Simple Chicken Fajita

Servings: 4
Cooking Time: 15 Minutes
Ingredients:

- 1 lb chicken breast, boneless, skinless & sliced
- 2 tsp olive oil
- 1 onion, sliced
- 2 bell peppers, sliced
- 1/8 tsp cayenne
- 1 tsp cumin
- 2 tsp chili powder
- Pepper
- Salt

Directions:

1. Add chicken, onion, and sliced bell peppers into the bowl.
2. Add cayenne, cumin, chili powder, oil, pepper, and salt and toss well.
3. Preheat the griddle to medium heat.
4. Add chicken mixture onto the hot griddle top and cook until vegetables are tender and chicken is cooked.
5. Serve and enjoy.

Nutrition Info: (Per Serving): Calories 185 ;Fat 5 g ;Carbohydrates 8.1 g ;Sugar 4.3 g ;Protein 25.2 g ;Cholesterol 73 mg

Flavorful Chicken Kababs

Servings: 3
Cooking Time: 15 Minutes
Ingredients:

- 2 chicken breasts, cut into cubes
- 1 onion, cut into quarters
- 1 bell pepper, cut into squares
- For marinade:
- 1 tsp nutmeg
- 1 tsp Italian seasoning
- 2 tsp sweet paprika

- 1/2 cup olive oil
- 1 lemon juice
- 2 garlic cloves, chopped
- 1/4 tsp cardamom
- 1/4 tsp paprika
- 1 tsp salt

Directions:

1. In a small bowl, mix together all marinade ingredients.
2. Add chicken, onions, and peppers in a large bowl.
3. Pour marinade over chicken and vegetables and coat well, cover, and place in the refrigerator for 1 hour.
4. Thread marinated chicken and vegetables onto the skewers.
5. Preheat the griddle to medium-low heat.
6. Spray griddle top with cooking spray.
7. Place skewers onto the hot griddle top and cook for 15 minutes or until chicken is cooked through. Turn skewers often.
8. Serve and enjoy.

Nutrition Info: (Per Serving): Calories 515 ;Fat 42 g ;Carbohydrates 8.2 g ;Sugar 4 g ;Protein 29 g ;Cholesterol 88 mg

Tasty Chicken Patties

Servings: 4
Cooking Time: 10 Minutes
Ingredients:
- 1 lb ground chicken
- 1/4 tsp red pepper flakes
- 1/2 tsp chili seasoning
- 1/2 tsp ground cumin
- 1 tsp paprika

Directions:

1. Add all ingredients into the large bowl and mix well to combine.
2. Make four small round patties from the mixture.
3. Preheat the griddle to high heat.
4. Spray griddle top with cooking spray.
5. Place patties on hot griddle top and cook for 5 minutes on each side.
6. Serve and enjoy.

Nutrition Info: (Per Serving): Calories 219 ;Fat 8 g ;Carbohydrates 0.8 g ;Sugar 0.1 g ;Protein 33 g ;Cholesterol 101 mg

Root Beer Can Chicken

Servings: 2 -4
Cooking Time: 20 Minutes
Ingredients:
- 1 lb. boneless chicken thighs
- 3 (12 ounce) cans root beer, like A&W
- Olive oil
- For the rub:
- 1 tablespoon garlic powder
- 3/4 tablespoon sea salt
- 1/2 tablespoon white pepper
- 2 teaspoons smoked paprika
- 2 teaspoons garlic powder
- 1 teaspoon dried thyme
- 1/8 teaspoon cayenne pepper

Directions:

1. Combine rub ingredients in a bowl; reserve half in a separate air tight container until ready to cook.
2. Rub chicken thighs evenly with olive oil and coat each with some rub.
3. Lay chicken in a 13 by 9 inch baking dish. Cover with 2 cans of root beer.
4. Preheat grill to medium-high heat.
5. Discard marinade and brush grill with olive oil.
6. Gently fold remaining rub and a half of the third can of root beer in a small bowl.
7. Sear chicken for 7 minutes on each side, basting often with root beer rub mix.
8. Serve when cooked through or chicken reaches 165°F and juices run clear.

Nutrition Info: Calories: 363, Sodium: 1185 mg, Dietary Fiber: 0.9g, Fat: 12.1g, Carbs: 29.9g, Protein: 33.4g.

Lemon Herb Chicken

Servings: 4
Cooking Time: 12 Minutes
Ingredients:
- 4 chicken breasts, skinless and boneless
- 1/4 tsp garlic powder

- 1/2 tsp cumin
- 1/2 tsp dried oregano
- 1/2 tsp dried basil
- 1 tbsp olive oil
- 1 tbsp fresh lemon juice
- 1/2 tsp granulated sugar
- Pepper
- Salt

Directions:

1. In a small bowl, mix basil, oregano, cumin, garlic powder, and sugar.
2. Brush chicken breasts with oil from both sides and season with dry seasoning mix.
3. Preheat the griddle to high heat.
4. Spray griddle top with cooking spray.
5. Place chicken on hot griddle top and cook for 5-6 minutes.
6. Turn chicken to other side and cook for 5-6 minutes more.
7. Transfer chicken to the serving plate and drizzle with lemon juice.
8. Serve and enjoy.

Nutrition Info: (Per Serving): Calories 310 ;Fat 14 g ;Carbohydrates 1 g ;Sugar 0.6 g ;Protein 42 g ;Cholesterol 130 mg

Buffalo Chicken Wings

Servings: 6 - 8
Cooking Time: 20 Minutes
Ingredients:

- 1 tablespoon sea salt
- 1 teaspoon ground black pepper
- 1 teaspoon garlic powder
- 3 lbs. chicken wings
- 6 tablespoons unsalted butter
- 1/3 cup buffalo sauce, like Moore's
- 1 tablespoon apple cider vinegar
- 1 tablespoon honey

Directions:

1. Combine salt, pepper and garlic powder in a large mixing bowl.
2. Toss the wings with the seasoning mixture to coat.
3. Preheat griddle to medium heat.
4. Place the wings on the griddle; make sure they are touching so the meat stays moist on the bone while grilling.
5. Flip wings every 5 minutes, for a total of 20 minutes of cooking.
6. Heat the butter, buffalo sauce, vinegar and honey in a saucepan over low heat; whisk to combine well.
7. Add wings to a large mixing bowl, toss the wings with the sauce to coat.
8. Turn griddle up to medium high and place wings back on the griddle until the skins crisp; about 1 to 2 minutes per side.
9. Add wings back into the bowl with the sauce and toss to serve.

Nutrition Info: Calories:410, Sodium: 950 mg, Dietary Fiber: 0.2 g, Fat: 21.3g, Carbs: 2.7g, Protein: 49.4g.

Healthy Chicken Fajitas

Servings: 4
Cooking Time: 15 Minutes
Ingredients:

- 2 chicken breasts, cut into chunks
- 2 carrots, sliced
- 2 zucchini, sliced
- 2 bell peppers, sliced
- 1 sweet potato, clean and cut into fries shape
- 1 tbsp olive oil
- 1/2 tsp dried oregano
- 1 tsp ground cumin
- 1 tbsp dried chives
- 2 tbsp paprika
- 1/4 tsp pepper
- 1 1/2 tsp salt

Directions:

1. Add all ingredients into the large mixing bowl and toss well.
2. Preheat the griddle to medium-low heat.
3. Spray griddle top with cooking spray.
4. Transfer chicken mixture onto the hot griddle top and cook until vegetables are tender and chicken is cooked.
5. Serve and enjoy.

Nutrition Info: (Per Serving): Calories 255 ;Fat 9.9 g ;Carbohydrates 19.1 g ;Sugar 8.4 g ;Protein 24.4 g ;Cholesterol 65 mg

Italian-style Sweet Pork Sausage With Fennel Seeds

Servings: 8
Cooking Time: 10 Minutes
Ingredients:
- 2½ pounds fatty boneless pork shoulder, cut into 1-inch cubes
- 3 cloves garlic, minced
- 1 tablespoon fennel seeds
- 1 teaspoon salt
- 1 teaspoon black pepper
- Sausage casings (optional)

Directions:
1. Preparing the Ingredients
2. Working in batches if necessary, put the meat in a food processor and pulse until coarsely ground— finer than chopped, but not much. Take your time and be careful not to pulverize the meat. As you finish each batch, transfer it to a bowl. Add the garlic, fennel seeds, salt, and pepper and work the mixture gently with your hands to incorporate them into the meat; add a little water if the mixture seems dry and crumbly. Cook up a spoonful in a small skillet to taste it; adjust the seasoning. Shape into 8 or more patties, or stuff into casings if you prefer. (You can freeze some or all of them, wrapped well, for up to several months.)
3. Bring the griddle grill to high heat. When the griddle is hot, put the sausages on the griddle, and cook until they release from the grates easily, 5 to 10 Minutes, then turn and cook the other side until the sausages are no longer pink in the center; the internal temperature should be 160°F (check with an instant-read thermometer, or nick with a small knife and peek inside). Transfer to a platter and serve.

Kale Caesar Salad With Seared Chicken

Servings: 1
Cooking Time: 8 Minutes
Ingredients:
- 1 chicken breast
- 1 teaspoon garlic powder
- ½ teaspoon black pepper
- ½ teaspoon sea salt
- 2 kale leaves, chopped
- shaved parmesan, for serving
- For the dressing:
- 1 tablespoon mayonnaise
- 1/2 tablespoon dijon mustard
- ½ teaspoon garlic powder
- 1/2 teaspoon worcestershire sauce
- 1/4 lemon, juice of (or 1/2 a small lime)
- ¼ teaspoon anchovy paste
- Pinch of sea salt
- Pinch of black pepper

Directions:
1. Mix garlic powder, black pepper, and sea salt in a small mixing bowl. Coat chicken with seasoning mix.
2. Preheat griddle to medium-high heat.
3. Sear chicken on each side for 7 minutes or until a meat thermometer reads 165°F when inserted in the thickest part of the breast.
4. Whisk all of the dressing ingredients together.
5. Plate your kale and pour the dressing over, and toss to combine.
6. Cut the chicken on a diagonal and place on top of the salad. Garnish with shaved parmesan, and serve.

Nutrition Info: Calories:643, Sodium:1549 mg, Dietary Fiber: 3.8 g, Fat: 18.6g, Carbs: 26.3g, Protein: 93.3g.

Teriyaki Chicken And Veggie Rice Bowls

Servings: 4
Cooking Time: 20 Minutes
Ingredients:
- 1 bag brown rice
- For the skewers:
- 2 boneless skinless chicken breasts, cubed
- 1 red onion, quartered
- 1 red pepper, cut into cube slices
- 1 green pepper, cut into cube slices
- 1/2 pineapple, cut into cubes
- For the marinade:
- 1/4 cup light soy sauce
- 1/4 cup sesame oil

- 1 tablespoon ginger, fresh grated
- 1 garlic clove, crushed
- 1/2 lime, juiced

Directions:

1. Whisk the marinade ingredients together in a small mixing bowl.
2. Add chicken and marinade to a resealable plastic bag, seal and toss well to coat.
3. Refrigerate for one hour or overnight.
4. Prepare rice as instructed on the bag.
5. Preheat the griddle to medium-high heat.
6. Thread the chicken and the cubed veggies onto 8 metal skewers and cook for 8 minutes on each side until seared and cooked through.
7. Portion rice out into bowls and top with two skewers each, and enjoy!

Nutrition Info: Calories: 477, Sodium:362 mg, Dietary Fiber: 3.8 g, Fat: 20.6g, Carbs:48.1g, Protein: 26.1g.

Salt-and-pepper Duck Breasts

Servings: 6

Cooking Time: 15 Minutes

Ingredients:

- 4 skin-on duck breasts (about 8 ounces each)
- Salt and pepper

Directions:

1. Preparing the Ingredients.
2. Trim the excess fat and skin from the duck without exposing the meat; reserve the scraps. With a sharp knife, cut slashes into the skin without slicing all the way down to the flesh; this will help render the fat as the duck cooks. Pat the duck dry with paper towels, then sprinkle both sides with salt and pepper.
3. Put the breasts in a cold large, heavy skillet, skin side down, along with the trimmings, and turn the heat to low. Let the breasts cook, rendering their fat, until the skin is golden brown and dry, 13 to 15 Minutes; the flesh side of the breast should still be cool or room temperature to the touch. Remove the breasts from the skillet. (At this point, you can let the breasts cool, cover them, and refrigerate for up to a day.)
4. Bring the griddle grill to high heat. When the griddle is hot, put the duck skin side up and cook until the breasts are one stage less done than you eventually want them, 3 to 10 Minutes; nick the thickest places with a small knife and peek inside. Turn the breasts over to let the skin crisp, just 1 to 2 Minutes. Transfer the duck breasts to a platter, let rest for 5 Minutes, slice, and serve with any accumulated juices.

Creole Chicken Stuffed With Cheese & Peppers

Servings: 4

Cooking Time: 20 Minutes

Ingredients:

- 4 boneless, skinless chicken breasts
- 8 mini sweet peppers, sliced thin and seeded
- 2 slices pepper jack cheese, cut in half
- 2 slices colby jack cheese, cut in half
- 1 tablespoon creole seasoning, like Emeril's
- 1 teaspoon black pepper
- 1 teaspoon garlic powder
- 1 teaspoon onion powder
- 4 teaspoons olive oil, separated
- Toothpicks

Directions:

1. Rinse chicken and pat dry.
2. Mix creole seasoning, pepper, garlic powder, and onion powder together in a small mixing bowl and set aside.
3. Cut a slit on the side of each chicken breast; be careful not to cut all the way through the chicken.
4. Rub each breast with 1 teaspoon each of olive oil.
5. Rub each chicken breast with seasoning mix and coat evenly.
6. Stuff each breast of chicken with 1 half pepper jack cheese slice, 1 half colby cheese slice, and a handful of pepper slices.
7. Secure chicken shut with 4 or 5 toothpicks.
8. Preheat the griddle to medium-high and cook chicken for 8 minutes per side; or until chicken reaches an internal temperature of 165°F.
9. Allow chicken to rest for 5 minutes, remove toothpicks, and serve.

Nutrition Info: Calories: 509, Sodium:1117 mg, Dietary Fiber: 3.4 g, Fat: 25.1g, Carbs: 19.8g, Protein: 51.4g.

Buffalo Chicken Panini

Servings: 4

Cooking Time: 4 Minutes

Ingredients:

- 2 cups shredded cooked chicken
- 1 large sweet onion, sliced
- 8 slices seedless rye
- 1/4 lb. thinly sliced Swiss cheese, about 8 slices
- 1/4 cup blue cheese dressing
- 1 cup mayonnaise
- 1 cup buffalo hot sauce
- 2 tbsps. unsalted butter
- blue cheese dressing

Directions:

1. Melt the butter in a large skillet on medium heat. Add the onions and cook for about 20 minutes.

2. Mix the buffalo sauce and mayonnaise in a medium bowl and toss with the chicken.

3. Put a slice of cheese on a piece of bread then the chicken, the onions and top with another slice of cheese and top with another piece of bread. Repeat the process with the remaining sandwiches. Spread the butter on the top and bottom of the sandwich

4. Preheat the Griddle Grill to Medium-High with unit closed.

5. Cook the sandwiches for 4 minutes, and make sure to check halfway through. The bread should be brown, and the cheese should be melted. Serve the sandwiches with a side of the blue cheese dressing.

Nutrition Info: (Per serving):Calories 387 Fat 11.3g, protein 9g, carbs 7g

BEEF, PORK AND LAMB RECIPES

Creole Pork Chops

Servings: 2
Cooking Time: 10 Minutes
Ingredients:

- 2 pork chops
- 2 tsp Creole seasoning
- 2 tbsp fresh parsley, chopped
- 1/4 tsp pepper
- Salt

Directions:

1. Season pork chops with Creole seasoning, pepper, and salt.
2. Preheat the griddle to high heat.
3. Spray griddle top with cooking spray.
4. Place seasoned pork chops on hot griddle top and cook for 5 minutes.
5. Turn pork chops and cook for 5 minutes more.
6. Transfer pork chops on serving plate and garnish with parsley.
7. Serve and enjoy.

Nutrition Info: (Per Serving): Calories 258 ;Fat 19 g ;Carbohydrates 0.4 g ;Sugar 0 g ;Protein 18 g ;Cholesterol 69 mg

Pork Baby Back Ribs

Servings: 4
Cooking Time: 2 Hours
Ingredients:

- 2 lbs. baby back ribs
- olive oil
- salt and pepper to taste
- BBQ sauce

Directions:

1. Remove the membrane from the bone side of the ribs. Coat with olive oil and sprinkle with salt and pepper. Let stand for 10 minutes.
2. Heat up the griddle grill to medium, and place the ribs bone side to the heat. Cook for 1.5 hours or until the temperature is 190–195 degrees.
3. Remove the ribs from the grill and let them relax for 30 minutes.
4. Brush the ribs with BBQ sauce, and place on a hot grill for 2–3 minutes to set the sauce before serving.

Nutrition Info: (Per serving):calories 290; fats 20g; carbohydrates 5g; Protein 23g

Chili-espresso Marinated Steak

Servings: 3
Cooking Time: 40 Minutes
Ingredients:

- ½ teaspoon garlic powder
- 1 ½ pounds beef flank steak
- 1 teaspoon instant espresso powder
- 2 tablespoons olive oil
- 2 teaspoons chili powder
- Salt and pepper to taste

Directions:

1. Preparing the Ingredients.
2. Make the dry rub by mixing the chili powder, salt, pepper, espresso powder, and garlic powder. Rub all over the steak and brush with oil.
3. Turn control knob to the high position, when the griddle is hot, place on the griddle and cook for 40 Minutes. Halfway through the cooking time, flip the beef to cook evenly.

Nutrition Info: (Per Serving): CALORIES: 249; FAT: 17G; PROTEIN:20G; FIBER:2G

Pork Tenderloin

Servings: 6
Cooking Time: 25 Minutes
Ingredients:

- pork tenderloin
- olive oil
- salt and pepper to taste

Directions:

1. Remove the silver skin and fat from the pork tenderloin and trim to a similar thickness.
2. Brush with olive oil and sprinkle with salt and pepper.
3. Heat up the griddle grill to high, and cook for 3–4 minutes per side or until the meat removes easily from the grill.

4. Remove the tenderloins from the grill and let them relax for several minutes.

5. Turn the griddle grill to medium and return the tenderloins to the grill. Cook for 15–20 minutes or until the temperature is 145 degrees.

6. Remove the tenderloins from the grill, and let them relax for several minutes before serving.

Nutrition Info: (Per serving): Calories: 122, Fat: 3g, Carbs: 8g, Protein: 22g

Grilled Beef Or Calf's Liver

Servings: 4
Cooking Time: 8 Minutes
Ingredients:
- 1–1½ pounds beef or calf's liver
- Salt and pepper
- Lemon wedges for serving

Directions:

1. Preparing the Ingredients

2. Slice the liver lengthwise into slices about ½ inch thick. Pat the slices dry with paper towels, then sprinkle with salt and pepper on both sides.

3. Turn control knob to the high position, when the griddle is hot, put the liver on the griddle and cook for 8 Minutes.

4. Transfer to a platter, let rest for 5 Minutes, then cut across into slices and serve with lemon wedges.

Cheesy Beef Patties

Servings: 6
Cooking Time: 12 Minutes
Ingredients:
- 2 lbs ground beef
- 1 tsp garlic powder
- 1 cup mozzarella cheese, grated
- 1 tsp onion powder
- Pepper
- Salt

Directions:

1. Add all ingredients into the large bowl and mix until well combined.

2. Preheat the griddle to high heat.

3. Spray griddle top with cooking spray.

4. Make patties from meat mixture and place onto the hot griddle top and cook until golden brown from both sides.

5. Serve and enjoy.

Nutrition Info: (Per Serving): Calories 295 ;Fat 10 g ;Carbohydrates 0.8 g ;Sugar 0.3 g ;Protein 47.3 g ;Cholesterol 138 mg

Beef Stir Fry

Servings: 4
Cooking Time: 10 Minutes
Ingredients:
- 1 lb steak, sliced
- 4 tbsp coconut oil
- 1/2 lb broccoli, cut into florets
- 1 tsp fish sauce
- 1 tsp sesame oil
- For marinade:
- 4 tbsp coconut aminos
- 2 garlic cloves, chopped
- 1 tsp ginger, grated

Directions:

1. Add sliced meat to a zip-lock bag with garlic, ginger, and coconut aminos and let marinate for 1 hour.

2. Blanch broccoli in boiling water for 2 minutes. Drain well.

3. Drain marinated meat.

4. Preheat the griddle to high heat.

5. Spray griddle top with cooking spray.

6. Add marinated meat onto the hot griddle top and cook for 1-3 minutes or until browned.

7. Add broccoli and stir fry for 3 minutes.

8. Add fish sauce and sesame oil and stir well.

9. Serve and enjoy.

Nutrition Info: (Per Serving): Calories 375 ;Fat 20 g ;Saturated fat 14 g ;Carbohydrates 4 g ;Sugar 1.1 g ;Protein 42.8 g ;Cholesterol 102 mg

Basic Juicy Ny Strip Steak

Servings: 1
Cooking Time: 8 Minutes
Ingredients:
- 1 (8 ounce) NY strip steak

- Olive oil
- Sea salt
- Fresh ground black pepper

Directions:
1. Remove the steak from the refrigerator and let it come to room temperature, about 30 to 45 minutes.
2. Preheat griddle to medium-high heat and brush with olive oil.
3. Season the steak on all sides with salt and pepper.
4. Cook steak about 4 to 5 minutes.
5. Flip and cook about 4 minutes more for medium rare steak; between 125°F and 130°F on a meat thermometer.
6. Transfer the steak to a plate and let it rest for 5 minutes before serving.

Nutrition Info: Calories:1560, Sodium: 8468 mg, Dietary Fiber: 0.g, Fat: 86g, Carbs: 0.1g Protein: 184g

Greek Lamb Patties

Servings: 4
Cooking Time: 8 Minutes
Ingredients:
- 1 lb ground lamb
- 5 basil leaves, minced
- 10 mint leaves, minced
- 1/4 cup fresh parsley, chopped
- 1 tsp dried oregano
- 1 cup feta cheese, crumbled
- 1 tbsp garlic, minced
- 1 jalapeno pepper, minced
- 1/4 tsp pepper
- 1/2 tsp kosher salt

Directions:
1. Add all ingredients into the mixing bowl and mix until well combined.
2. Preheat the griddle to high heat.
3. Spray griddle top with cooking spray.
4. Make four equal shape patties from meat mixture and place onto the hot griddle top and cook for 4 minutes on each side.
5. Serve and enjoy.

Nutrition Info: (Per Serving): Calories 317 ;Fat 16.4 g ;Carbohydrates 3 g ;Sugar 1.7 g ;Protein 37.5 g ;Cholesterol 135 mg

Beef Salad With Fresh Mint

Servings: 4
Cooking Time: 8 Minutes
Ingredients:
- 4 cups torn Boston or romaine lettuce
- leaves, mesclun, or any salad greens
- mixture
- 1 cup torn fresh mint leaves
- ½ small red onion, cut into thin julienne
- 1 cucumber, peeled, seeded if necessary, and cut into thin julienne
- 1 carrot, peeled and cut into thin julienne
- Juice of 2 limes
- 2 tablespoons soy sauce
- 2 tablespoons rice vinegar
- 1 tablespoon sugar
- 1 jalapeño chile, seeded if you like, thinly sliced
- Salt and pepper
- 1½ pounds boneless steak

Directions:
1. Preparing the Ingredients
2. Put the lettuce, mint, onion, cucumber, and carrot in a large bowl. Whisk the lime juice, soy sauce, vinegar, sugar, jalapeño, and 1 tablespoon water together in a small bowl; the mixture will be thin. Taste and add salt and pepper if you like. (You can prepare the salad and dressing up to several hours in advance; refrigerate both until you're ready to serve; drape a damp kitchen towel over the vegetables to keep them fresh.)
3. Pat the steak dry with paper towels, then sprinkle with salt and pepper on both sides.
4. Turn control knob to the high position, when the griddle is hot, add cooking oil and when it begins to shimmer, place the steak on the griddle and cook for 8 Minutes.
5. Transfer to a cutting board and let rest while you dress the salad; check the temperature of the meat occasionally. (Or nick with a small knife and peek inside.)
6. Transfer 2 tablespoons of the dressing to a medium-sized bowl. Drizzle the rest of the dressing over the salad and toss to coat. Transfer the salad to a platter if you like.

7.   Thinly slice the steak across the grain. Put the beef and any accumulated juices in the bowl with the reserved dressing and toss to combine. Scatter the steak slices over the salad, drizzle with the juices, and serve.

5.   Divide the slices among 4 plates and drizzle with a spoonful of the reserved sauce. Squeeze some lime juice over each portion and serve immediately.
Nutrition Info: (Per Serving): CALORIES:350; FAT: 16G; PROTEIN:38G

Spicy Soy Flank Steak

Servings: 4
Cooking Time: 5 Minutes
Ingredients:
- SPICY SOY SAUCE
- 1 tablespoon olive oil
- 1 tablespoon minced garlic
- 1 tablespoon minced fresh ginger
- ½ cup low-sodium soy sauce
- 2 tablespoons dark brown sugar
- ½ teaspoon red pepper flakes
- Heat the olive oil in a small saucepan over medium heat. Add the garlic and ginger and, stirring frequently, cook until the garlic begins to brown, about 2 Minutes. Add the soy sauce, sugar, and red pepper flakes and bring to a simmer. Cook, stirring occasionally, until a thick glaze forms, about 10 Minutes. (The sauce can be cooled, covered, and refrigerated overnight. Reheat before serving.)
- FLANKSTEAK
- 1½ pounds flank steak, about 1 inch thick
- ¼ teaspoon salt
- ½ teaspoon freshly ground black pepper
- 1 lime, cut into wedges

Directions:
1.   Preparing the Ingredients
2.   Pour half of the spicy soy sauce into a small bowl to use as a glaze. Put the remaining sauce aside.
3.   Season the steak on both sides with the salt and pepper. Brush both sides of the steak with some of the sauce from the small bowl.
4.   Turn control knob to the high position, when the griddle is hot, add cooking oil, and when it begins to shimmer, grill the steak for 2 Minutes, then brush the top of the steak with the rest of the sauce in the bowl. Grill for about 3 Minutes more for medium-rare. It should have grill marks and feel fairly firm to the touch. Let the steak rest on a cutting board for about 5 Minutes before slicing, thinly, across the grain.

Tender Steak With Pineapple Rice

Servings: 4
Cooking Time: 10 Minutes
Ingredients:
- 4 (4-ounce) beef fillets
- ¼ cup soy sauce
- ½ teaspoon black pepper
- ½ teaspoon garlic powder
- 1 (8-ounce) can pineapple chunks, in juice, drained
- 2 scallions, thin sliced
- 2 (8.8-ounce) packages pre-cooked brown rice, like Uncle Ben's
- 7/8 teaspoon kosher salt
- Olive oil, for brushing

Directions:
1.   Combine soy sauce, pepper, garlic powder, and beef in a large sealable plastic bag.
2.   Seal and massage sauce into beef; let stand at room temperature for 7 minutes, turning bag occasionally.
3.   Preheat griddle to medium-high heat and brush with olive oil.
4.   Add pineapple and green onions to grill and cook 5 minutes or until well charred, turning to char evenly.
5.   Remove pineapple mix and brush with additional olive oil.
6.   Add steaks and cook 3 minutes on each side, for rare, or until desired temperature is reached.
7.   Cook rice according to package instructions.
8.   Add rice, pineapple, onions, and salt to a bowl and stir gently to combine.
9.   Plate steaks with pineapple rice and serve!
Nutrition Info: Calories: 369, Sodium: 1408 mg, Dietary Fiber: 2.1g, Fat: 12.4g, Carbs: 37g Protein: 27.9g

Marinated London Broil

Servings: 4
Cooking Time: 4 Minutes
Ingredients:
- 2-lb. London broil
- MARINADE
- ½ cup soy sauce
- 2 Tbsp. balsamic vinegar
- 2 Tbsp. Dijon mustard
- 4 cloves garlic, minced
- 2 Tbsp. olive oil
- 3 sprigs fresh rosemary
- 1 tsp. coarsely ground black pepper

Directions:
1. Preparing the Ingredients
2. Combine all marinade ingredients in mixing bowl and whisk together.
3. Using a sharp knife, cut a diamond, or crosshatch, pattern into each side of the meat, only cutting about ¼ inch deep. This will allow the marinade to penetrate the meat deeper in a shorter amount of time.
4. Place meat in sealable plastic bag and cover with marinade. Place in refrigerator for 2 hours. After 2 hours, remove from refrigerator and allow to come up to room temperature for 1 hour.
5. Remove meat from marinade and pat dry with paper towel.
6. Turn control knob to the high position. Oil the griddle and allow it to heat until the oil is shimmering but not smoking. Let cook for 2 Minutes, rotate 90 degrees, and allow to cook for another 2 Minutes.
7. Flip meat and repeat.
8. Remove from grill when internal temperature reaches 125°F. Tent with foil and let rest for 5 Minutes before slicing.
9. Serve with chipotle aioli.

Easy Lemon Pepper Pork Chops

Servings: 4
Cooking Time: 12 Minutes
Ingredients:
- 4 pork chops, boneless
- 1 tsp lemon pepper seasoning
- Salt

Directions:
1. Preheat the griddle to high heat.
2. Spray griddle top with cooking spray.
3. Season pork chops with lemon pepper seasoning, and salt and place onto the hot griddle top and cook for 5-7 minutes per side.
4. Serve and enjoy.

Nutrition Info: (Per Serving): Calories 257 ;Fat 20 g ;Carbohydrates 0.3 g ;Sugar 0 g ;Protein 18 g ;Cholesterol 69 mg

Romanian Garlic Steak

Servings: 6
Cooking Time: 10 Minutes
Ingredients:
- 8 cloves garlic, minced
- 1 teaspoon salt
- Juice of 1 lemon
- 1½ to 2 pounds flank steak
- ¼ cup good-quality olive oil

Directions:
1. Preparing the Ingredients
2. To make the marinade, combine half the garlic with the salt and lemon juice in a small bowl.
3. Put the steak in a large shallow baking dish and work the marinade into it on both sides, using your hands to massage it evenly all over the steak. Let sit at room temperature while you prepare the fire. Or cover and refrigerate for several hours or overnight.
4. Whisk the remainder of the garlic and the oil together in another small bowl with a fork, pressing down on the garlic as you work.
5. Remove the steak from the marinade and let any excess drip off.
6. Turn control knob to the high position, when the griddle is hot, add cooking oil and when it begins to shimmer, put the steak on the griddle and cook for 5 Minutes for medium-rare. Flip and sear for an additional 1 to 3 Minutes, based on your desired doneness.
7. Transfer to a cutting board and let rest for 5 to 10 Minutes, checking the internal temperature. (Or nick with a small knife and peek inside.) Slice thinly across the grain, transfer to a platter, pour over any

accumulated juices, and serve with the garlic oil on the side to drizzle over.

Steak & Mushrooms

Servings: 4
Cooking Time: 15 Minutes
Ingredients:

- 1 lb steaks, cut into 1-inch cubes
- 8 oz mushrooms, halved
- 1/2 tsp garlic powder
- 1 tsp Worcestershire sauce
- 2 tbsp olive oil
- Pepper
- Salt

Directions:
1. Add steak cubes and remaining ingredients into the bowl and toss well.
2. Preheat the griddle to high heat.
3. Transfer meat mixture onto the hot griddle top and stir fry until meat is completely cooked.
4. Serve and enjoy.
Nutrition Info: (Per Serving): Calories 300 ;Fat 12 g ;Carbohydrates 2.4 g ;Sugar 1.3 g ;Protein 42.8 g ;Cholesterol 102 mg

Thick Stacked Sizzling Burgers On The Griddle

Servings: 6
Cooking Time: 8 Minutes
Ingredients:

- 1-1/2 pounds ground beef, 80% to 85% lean
- 6 hamburger buns
- 1/4 stick butter (use oil as substitute if desired)
- Pinch salt
- Pinch fresh black pepper
- 6 slices cheese
- Burger toppings:
- 2 sliced tomatoes,
- 1/4 onion (sliced)
- 2 pickles
- 3 tbsp. Ketchup
- 2 tbsp. Mustard
- 6 lettuce leaves

Directions:
1. Preheat Griddle Grill to Sear with the unit closed.
2. Shape ground beef into 6 big and chunky patties, then melt butter on griddle over medium heat. Lightly butter the buns, then toasting them to your desired liking. Move the buns to a clean plate. Then, using the same pan, cook the patties for several minutes. Add a pinch of salt and pepper to each and continue to cook for 3 to 4 min.
3. Flip the burgers and repeat the process, adding a little more salt and pepper than before. Cook for another several minutes or until cooked to your desired liking.
Nutrition Info: (Per serving):calories 980; fats 43g; Carbs 13.3 g; protein 9g

Ranch Pork Chops

Servings: 6
Cooking Time: 15 Minutes
Ingredients:

- 6 pork chops, boneless
- 2 tbsp ranch seasoning, homemade
- 1/4 cup olive oil
- 1 tsp dried parsley
- Pepper
- Salt

Directions:
1. Preheat the griddle to high heat.
2. Spray griddle top with cooking spray.
3. Season pork chops with pepper and salt and place onto the hot griddle top.
4. Mix together olive oil, parsley, and ranch seasoning.
5. Spoon oil mixtures over pork chops and cook pork chops for 5-7 minutes per side.
6. Serve and enjoy.
Nutrition Info: (Per Serving): Calories 328 ;Fat 28.3 g ;Carbohydrates 0 g ;Sugar 0 g ;Protein 18 g ;Cholesterol 69 mg

Steak With Green Chimichurri

Servings: 5
Cooking Time: 10 Minutes
Ingredients:

- 2 cups packed fresh parsley leaves
- 3 cloves garlic, peeled
- ¼ cup good-quality olive oil
- 2 tablespoons red wine vinegar
- ½ teaspoon red chile flakes, or more to
- taste
- Salt and pepper
- 1½ to 2 pounds flank or skirt steak

Directions:

1. Preparing the Ingredients
2. Put the parsley, garlic, oil, vinegar, red pepper, and a sprinkle of salt in a blender or food processor and purée. Taste and adjust the seasonings as needed. Transfer to a small serving bowl. (You can prepare the sauce several hours ahead; cover and refrigerate.)
3. Pat the meat dry with paper towels and sprinkle with salt and pepper on both sides.
4. Bring the griddle grill to high heat. When the griddle is hot, add cooking oil, and when it begins to shimmer add the steak and cook for 10 Minutes for medium-rare flank steak.
5. Transfer to a cutting board and let rest 5 to 10 Minutes, checking the internal temperature. (Or nick with a small knife and peek inside.) Slice thinly across the grain, transfer to a platter, pour over any accumulated juices, and serve with the chimichurri on the side.

Boston Strip Steak And Blue Cheese Butter

Servings: 3
Cooking Time: 5 Minutes
Ingredients:

- 2 tsp. olive oil
- 1 large Vidalia onion, sliced
- 1 tsp. Worcestershire sauce
- 2 to 4 (8-oz.) Boston strip steaks
- ½ tsp. sea salt per steak
- 1 Tbsp. roasted garlic and blue cheese butter per steak

Directions:

1. Preparing the Ingredients
2. Turn control knob to the high position. Add cooking oil and when it begins to shimmer, sauté onions, adding Worcestershire sauce after onions have cooked for 5 Minutes.

3. Prepare each steak by sprinkling each with ½ teaspoon of sea salt.
4. Place steaks on hot griddle. Grill for 2 Minutes, rotate 90 degrees, and grill for an additional 2 Minutes.
5. Flip steak and repeat, removing from grill when internal temperature reaches 125°F
6. Serve over sautéed onions, and top with 1 tablespoon of roasted garlic and blue cheese butter.

Ham Steak With Spicy Pineapple Glaze

Servings: 6
Cooking Time: 15 Minutes
Ingredients:

- ¼ cup pineapple preserves
- 2 tablespoons brown sugar
- 1 tablespoon hot sauce, or to taste
- 1 or 2 center-cut bone-in ham steaks (1–1½ inches thick; about 2 pounds)

Directions:

1. Preparing the Ingredients.
2. To make the glaze, stir the preserves, brown sugar, and hot sauce together in a small bowl.
3. Bring the griddle grill to high heat. When the griddle is hot, put the ham steak(s) on the griddle, and cook for 10 Minutes. Brush the top with the glaze and turn again; brush the top with glaze as well. Cook until the glaze on the bottom starts to brown (this will only take a minute or 2). Brush the top with glaze again and cook until the other side starts to brown. Continue building up the glaze until the steak is hot throughout and browned and crusted on both sides.
4. Transfer to a cutting board, slice, and serve.

Bacon-wrapped Pork Medallions

Servings: 4
Cooking Time: 15 Minutes
Ingredients:

- 1½ pounds pork tenderloin, trimmed of excess fat and silverskin.
- Salt and pepper
- 8 ounces sliced bacon

Directions:

1. Preparing the Ingredients.
2. Pat the meat dry with paper towels. Sprinkle with salt and pepper on all sides.
3. Cut the tenderloin across into medallions so that their thickness matches the width of the bacon slices. Pat dry with paper towels and sprinkle with salt and pepper on both sides. Wrap a piece of bacon around the outside of the medallion and secure it with a toothpick. Repeat for the remaining medallions. Or you can secure the bacon by running two skewers parallel through the medallions, with several medallions on each pair of skewers.
4. Bring the griddle grill to high heat. When the griddle is hot, put the medallions on the griddle, and cook until the bacon has browned and the pork is slightly pink in the center (an internal temperature of 140°F), 10 to 15 Minutes total.
5. Transfer to a platter, let rest about 5 Minutes, until the internal temperature rises to 145°F. Serve.

Glazed Country Ribs

Servings: 6
Cooking Time: 4 Hours
Ingredients:
- 3 pounds country-style pork ribs
- 1 cup low-sugar ketchup
- ½ cup water
- ¼ cup onion, finely chopped
- ¼ cup cider vinegar or wine vinegar
- ¼ cup light molasses
- 2 tablespoons Worcestershire sauce
- 2 teaspoons chili powder
- 2 cloves garlic, minced

Directions:
1. Combine ketchup, water, onion, vinegar, molasses, Worcestershire sauce, chili powder, and garlic in a saucepan and bring to boil; reduce heat. Simmer, uncovered, for 10 to 15 minutes or until desired thickness is reached, stirring often.
2. Trim fat from ribs.
3. Preheat griddle to medium-high.
4. Place ribs, bone-side down, on griddle and cook for 1-1/2 to 2 hours or until tender, brushing occasionally with sauce during the last 10 minutes of cooking.

5. Serve with remaining sauce and enjoy!
Nutrition Info: Calories: 404, Sodium: 733 mg, Dietary Fiber: 0.4g, Fat: 8.1g, Carbs:15.2g Protein: 60.4g

Succulent Griddle-seared Garlic Tenderloin

Servings: 2
Cooking Time: 8 Minutes
Ingredients:
- 12 oz. steaks (can use 2 6oz. flat iron tenderloin)
- 1 tbsp. Olive oil
- 1/2 teaspoon garlic powder
- 1/2 teaspoon onion powder
- 1/2 teaspoon black pepper
- 1 pinch of salt (to taste)

Directions:
1. Preheat Griddle Grill to Medium-High with the unit closed.
2. After bringing steak to room temperature, pat the meat with a paper towel to remove moisture. Season with the salt, pepper, onion and garlic powders.
3. Add oil to your griddle.
4. Let the steaks cook for a few minutes turning them over and repeating after first side is cooked, then flip and cook for another 3 minutes. Turn over the steaks and cook for another 2 to 3 minutes. Check steaks to see if they are cooked to your liking, but each side should be at least brown in color.
5. Slice and serve the steak after letting it cool for several minutes.
Nutrition Info: (Per serving):Calories 667kcal; protein47 g; carbs18g; fat 20g

Molasses Bbq Pork Chops

Servings: 4
Cooking Time: 4 Minutes
Ingredients:
- MOLASSES BARBECUE SAUCE
- 2 tablespoons molasses
- 2 tablespoons ketchup
- 1 tablespoon cider vinegar
- 1 teaspoon light brown sugar

- ¼ teaspoon salt
- Pinch of ground cloves
- Pinch of sweet paprika
- PORK
- 4 (6-ounce) boneless center-cut pork
- chops, pounded to ½-inch thickness

Directions:

1. Preparing the Ingredients
2. Whisk together the molasses, ketchup, vinegar, brown sugar, salt, cloves, and paprika in a small bowl. (The sauce can be covered with plastic wrap and refrigerated for up to 3 days.)
3. Pour the sauce into a shallow baking dish. Add the chops and turn to coat. Bring the griddle grill to high heat. When the griddle is hot, grill the chops for about 4 Minutes, until they have taken on grill marks and are firm to the touch. Serve immediately.

Nutrition Info: (Per Serving): CALORIES: 283; FAT: 4G; PROTEIN:37G

Griddle Baked Beef Stew

Servings: 8
Cooking Time: 5 Hours
Ingredients:
- 2-1/2 lbs. beef stew meat chunks
- 8 carrots, chopped
- 3 medium white onions, quartered
- 5 medium white potatoes, quartered
- 2 cans Sweet Peas
- 2 bay leaves
- 2 beef bouillon cubes
- 1 tbsp. sugar
- 1 tbsp. salt
- 1/4 tbsp. thyme
- 1 tbsp. black pepper
- 1/4 cup cornstarch
- 1 (28-oz.) can whole tomatoes
- 1 cup water

Directions:

1. Preheat the griddle to medium high.
2. Pour all the ingredients in a Skillet and set on the griddle.
3. Cover and cook for 5 hours, stir once or twice
4. Serve immediately and enjoy.

Nutrition Info: (Per serving):calories 439kcal, fat 13g, carbs50g, protein30g

Caprese Flank Steak

Servings: 4
Cooking Time: 10 Minutes
Ingredients:
- 4 (6 ounce) flank steaks
- Sea salt, for seasoning
- Flakey sea salt, for serving
- Fresh ground pepper
- Olive oil
- 2 roma tomatoes, sliced
- 4 ounces fresh buffalo mozzarella, cut into four slices
- 8 fresh basil leaves
- Balsamic vinegar glaze, for drizzling

Directions:

1. Lightly brush each filet, on all sides, with olive oil and season with salt and pepper.
2. Preheat griddle to high. Place steaks on griddle, reduce heat to medium, tent with foil and cook for 5 minutes.
3. Flip, re-tent, and cook for an additional 5 minutes; during the last 2 minutes of cooking, top each with a slice of mozzarella.
4. Remove steaks from the griddle and top each with a few tomato slices, 2 basil leafs.
5. Drizzle with balsamic glaze, and sprinkle with flakey salt and a little more black pepper.

Nutrition Info: Calories: 461, Sodium:485 mg, Dietary Fiber: 0.8g, Fat: 22.8g, Carbs: 5.7g Protein: 55.9g

Garlic Soy Pork Chops

Servings: 4 - 6
Cooking Time: 1 Hour
Ingredients:
- 4 to 6 pork chops
- 4 cloves garlic, finely chopped
- 1/2 cup olive oil
- 1/2 cup soy sauce
- 1/2 teaspoon garlic powder
- 1/2 teaspoon salt

- 1/2 black pepper
- 1/4 cup butter

Directions:

1. In a large zipperlock bag, combine the garlic, olive oil, soy sauce, and garlic powder. Add the pork chops and make sure the marinade coats the chops. Set aside for 30 minutes.

2. Heat your griddle to medium-high heat. Add 2 tablespoons of olive oil and 2 tablespoons of butter to the griddle.

3. Add the chops to the griddle one at a time, making sure they are not crowded. Add another 2 tablespoons of butter to the griddle and cook the chops for 4 minutes. Cook an additional 4 minutes.

4. Remove the chops from the griddle and spread the remaining butter over them. Serve after resting for 5 minutes.

Nutrition Info: Calories: 398 Sodium: 1484 mg, Dietary Fiber: 0.2g, Fat: 37.7g, Carbs: 2.5g Protein: 13.6g

Grilled Stuffed Pork Tenderloin

Servings: 4
Cooking Time: 30 Minutes
Ingredients:

- 1½ Tbsp. olive oil, plus a drizzle
- ½ medium Vidalia onion, finely chopped
- 1 tsp. Worcestershire sauce
- 6 oz. chopped baby bella mushrooms
- 2 cloves garlic, minced
- 2 tsp. minced rosemary
- 4 fresh sage leaves, chopped
- ½ tsp. celery salt
- ½ tsp. fresh black pepper
- ¼ cup chopped flat-leaf parsley
- 2 cups fresh spinach leaves, stems
- removed
- 2 tsp. Dijon mustard
- 1 pork tenderloin, 1½ to 2 lb.
- 4 slices pancetta
- 4 slices provolone cheese
- 2 tsp. rosemary salt

Directions:

1. Preparing the Ingredients

2. In a medium skillet, heat olive oil over medium heat. Add onion and cook for 1 minute before adding Worcestershire sauce, mushrooms, garlic, rosemary, sage, celery salt, and black pepper. Constantly mixing with wooden spoon, cook down till mushrooms are soft (5–7 Minutes).

3. Add parsley and spinach. Continue to mix with wooden spoon. Cook until spinach starts to wilt. Stir in mustard and cook for additional 1 minute. Remove from heat, set aside, and allow to cool while you prep the pork.

4. Place pork tenderloin on cutting board, and with your knife parallel to the cutting surface, roll cut the tenderloin so it's about ½-inch thick when unrolled.

5. Once pork has been roll cut, lay pancetta on top, followed by provolone cheese and spinach mixture. Leave about a 1-inch border around the edge of the loin.

6. Roll tenderloin back up and truss together with butcher's twine. (If you're not sure how to truss, just tie the roll up using a simple square knot every 2 inches, but trussing is super easy.

7. Drizzle outside of roll with a very thin coat of olive oil and sprinkle with rosemary salt.

8. Bring the griddle grill to high heat. When the griddle is hot, place the pork on the griddle grill and cook for 11 Minutes. After 11 Minutes, flip the pork, and cook for an additional 11 Minutes.

9. Remove from grill, slice, and serve.

Hibachi Steak

Servings: 4
Cooking Time: 5 Minutes
Ingredients:

- 2 Lbs. Tri-Tip Beef, Cut Into 1/8-Inch Slices
- 1/2 Cup Teriyaki Sauce
- 1 Tsp. Fresh Grated Ginger
- 2 Cloves Garlic, Minced
- 1/4 Cup Brown Sugar
- 2 Tbsp. Worcestershire Sauce
- 3 Tsp. Black Pepper

Directions:

1. Mix all the ingredients together in a covered bowl or resealable bag, and refrigerate for several hours to overnight.

2. Heat the griddle grill to high and grill for about 1 minute per side until cooked through.

3. Let rest for several minutes before serving.

Nutrition Info: (Per serving): Calories: 451, Carbs: 2g, Fats: 32g, Protein: 37g

Grill Pork Quesadilla

Servings: 2
Cooking Time: 12 Minutes

Ingredients:

- Two 6-inch corn or flour tortilla shells
- 1 medium-sized pork shoulder, approximately 4 ounces, sliced
- ½ medium-sized white onion, sliced
- ½ medium-sized red pepper, sliced
- ½ medium sized green pepper, sliced
- ½ medium sized yellow pepper, sliced
- ¼ cup of shredded pepper-jack cheese
- ¼ cup of shredded mozzarella cheese

Directions:

1. Preparing the Ingredients.

2. Bring the griddle grill to high heat. When the griddle is hot, grill the pork, onion, and peppers in foil in the griddle grill, allowing the moisture from the vegetables and the juice from the pork mingle together. Remove pork and vegetables. While they're cooling, sprinkle half the shredded cheese over one of the tortillas, then cover with the pieces of pork, onions, and peppers, and then layer on the rest of the shredded cheese. Top with the second tortilla. Place directly on hot surface of the griddle.

3. Set the temperature to MED. After 6 Minutes, flip the tortillas onto the other side with a spatula; the cheese should be melted enough that it won't fall apart, but be careful anyway not to spill any toppings.

4. Reset to HIGH for another 6 Minutes.

5. After 6 Minutes, the tortillas should be browned and crisp, and the pork, onion, peppers and cheese will be crispy and hot and delicious. Remove with tongs and let sit on a serving plate to cool for a few Minutes before slicing.

Coffee Crusted Skirt Steak

Servings: 8

Cooking Time: 20 Minutes

Ingredients:

- 1/4 cup coffee beans, finely ground
- 1/4 cup dark brown sugar, firmly packed
- 1 1/2 teaspoon sea salt
- 1/8 teaspoon ground cinnamon
- Pinch cayenne pepper
- 2 1/2 lb. skirt steak, cut into 4 pieces
- 1 tablespoon olive oil

Directions:

1. Heat griddle to high.

2. Combine coffee, brown sugar, salt, cinnamon, and cayenne pepper in a bowl to make rub.

3. Remove steak from refrigerator and let come to room temperature, about 15 minutes. Rub steak with oil, and sprinkle with spice rub. Massage spice rub into meat.

4. Sear until charred and medium-rare, 2 to 4 minutes per side. Transfer to a cutting board, cover with foil and let rest 5 minutes before thinly slicing against the grain.

Nutrition Info: Calories:324, Sodium: 461 mg, Dietary Fiber: 0.1g, Fat: 16g, Carbs: 4.6g Protein: 37.9g

Greek Flank Steak Gyros

Servings: 4
Cooking Time: 20 Minutes

Ingredients:

- 1 pound flank steak
- 1 white onion, thinly sliced
- 1 roma tomato, thinly sliced
- 1 cucumber, peeled and thinly sliced
- 1/4 cup crumbled feta cheese
- 4 6-inch pita pockets
- For the marinade:
- 1/4 cup olive oil, plus more for brushing
- 1 teaspoon dried oregano
- 1 teaspoon balsamic vinegar
- 1 teaspoon garlic powder
- Sea salt and freshly ground pepper, to taste
- For the sauce:
- 1 cup plain yogurt
- 2 tablespoons fresh dill (can use dried), chopped
- 1 teaspoon garlic, minced

- 2 tablespoons lemon juice

Directions:

1. Cut the flank steak into thin strips against the grain. Add the marinade ingredients to a large sealable plastic bag, add the sliced meat, seal, and turn to coat.
2. Place in the refrigerator to marinate for 2 hours or overnight.
3. Preheat the griddle to medium-high heat, and an oven to 250°F.
4. Combine the sauce ingredients in small mixing bowl and set aside.
5. Spritz the pitas with a little water, wrap in foil and place in the oven to warm.
6. Brush griddle with olive oil.
7. Add meat to grill and discard marinade. Cook until brown and cooked through, about 5 minutes.
8. Remove the pitas from the oven, and cut in half.
9. Arrange the pitas on plates and stuff with cucumber, tomato, onions, and beef.
10. Spoon some yogurt sauce over the meat and top with feta and serve.

Nutrition Info: Calories:901, Sodium: 1221 mg, Dietary Fiber: 5.7g, Fat: 27.2g, Carbs:107.8g Protein: 53.5g

Filipino-style Pork Skewers

Servings: 4

Cooking Time: 20 Minutes

Ingredients:

- 2 pounds boneless pork shoulder
- ½ cup ginger beer
- 2 tablespoons soy sauce
- 2 tablespoons ketchup
- 2 tablespoons brown sugar
- 1 tablespoon minced garlic
- 1 tablespoon fresh lime juice
- Salt and pepper

Directions:

1. Preparing the Ingredients.
2. Trim the pork of excess fat and cut into 1-to 1½-inch pieces.
3. Put the ginger beer, soy sauce, ketchup, sugar, garlic, lime juice, and some salt and pepper in a large bowl and whisk to combine. Add the pork and stir to

coat. Let sit at room temperature while you prepare the fire or up to 1 hour. Or refrigerate up to overnight.

4. If you're using bamboo or wooden skewers, soak them in water for 30 Minutes.
5. Skewer the pork; you can push the pieces close together. Bring the griddle grill to high heat. When the griddle is hot, put the skewers on the griddle, and cook until crusty brown and no longer pink in the center; turn the skewers. Total cooking time will be about 20 Minutes. Transfer the skewers to a platter and serve.

Pork Chimichurri

Servings: 4

Cooking Time: 10 Minutes

Ingredients:

- CHIMI CHURRI SAUCE
- 1 large red onion, cut into ½-inch slices
- 2 red bell peppers, cored, seeded, and cut into 1-inch strips
- 2 yellow bell peppers, cored, seeded, and cut into 1-inch strips
- 3 tablespoons olive oil
- 2 tablespoons white wine vinegar
- Juice of 1 lime
- 1 teaspoon Worcestershire sauce
- ½ teaspoon red pepper flakes
- 2 tablespoons chopped fresh parsley leaves
- PORK
- 2 pounds pork tenderloin
- 1 tablespoon olive oil
- ¼ teaspoon salt
- ½ teaspoon freshly ground black pepper

Directions:

1. Preparing the Ingredients
2. Toss the onion slices and bell pepper strips in 2 tablespoons of the olive oil to coat them lightly. Bring the griddle grill to high heat. When the griddle is hot, grill the onion and peppers for about 6 Minutes, until soft and charred.
3. Finely chop the peppers and onion in a food processor or by hand using a large sharp knife. Transfer to a medium bowl. Stir in the remaining tablespoon olive oil, the vinegar, lime juice,

Worcestershire sauce, and red pepper flakes. (The sauce can be covered with plastic wrap and refrigerated for up to 2 days. Bring to room temperature before serving.) Stir in the parsley just before serving.

4.   Cut the pork tenderloin into 8 medallions, each about 1 inch thick, and then pound them to a ½-inch thickness. Rub the pork cutlets with the olive oil and season with the salt and pepper. Grill for about 3 Minutes, until the cutlets have taken on grill marks and are firm to the touch. Serve each person 2 cutlets with the sauce heaped on top.

Nutrition Info: (Per Serving): CALORIES: 446; FAT: 22G; PROTEIN:49G

Apple Cider Pork Chops

Servings: 4
Cooking Time: 3 Minutes
Ingredients:
- 2 cups water
- 1 cup apple cider
- 1 small onion, roughly chopped
- 1 apple, roughly chopped
- ¼ cup salt
- ¼ cup light brown sugar
- 3 whole peppercorns
- 3 fresh thyme sprigs or ½ teaspoon dried thyme
- 4 (6-ounce) boneless center-cut pork chops, pounded to ½-inch thickness

Directions:
1.   Preparing the Ingredients
2.   Combine all of the ingredients except the pork chops in a bowl large enough to hold all of the chops. Stir until the salt and brown sugar dissolve. Add the chops to the brine. Cover with plastic wrap and refrigerate overnight or for up to 24 hours.
3.   Bring the griddle grill to high heat. When the griddle is hot, grill the pork chops for about 3 Minutes, until the meat has taken on grill marks and is firm to the touch.
4.   Serve immediately.

Nutrition Info: (Per Serving): CALORIES: 244; FAT: 12G; PROTEIN:32G

Lemon Pepper London Broil

Servings: 4
Cooking Time: 10 Minutes
Ingredients:
- 1 flank steak or piece of sirloin or top or bottom round steak (1½ to 1¾ pounds)
- 1 tablespoon cracked black peppercorns
- 2 teaspoons finely grated lemon zest
- 3 cloves garlic, coarsely chopped
- 1 shallot, coarsely chopped
- 3 tablespoons soy sauce
- 1 tablespoon Dijon mustard
- 1 tablespoon fresh lemon juice
- 2 tablespoons vegetable oil

Directions:
1.   Preparing the Ingredients
2.   If using flank steak, score it on both sides in a crosshatch pattern, making shallow cuts on the diagonal no deeper than ⅛ inch and about ¼ inch apart. This will keep the flank steak from curling as it cooks; you don't have to score sirloin or top or bottom round.
3.   Place the peppercorns, lemon zest, garlic, and shallot in a food processor and process to a coarse paste. Add the soy sauce, mustard, lemon juice, and 1 tablespoon of the oil. Spread half of the soy sauce mixture in the bottom of a baking dish just large enough to hold the beef. Place the meat on top and spread the remaining soy sauce mixture over it. Let the meat marinate for at least 4 hours or as long as overnight. You can also marinate the beef in a resealable plastic bag.
4.   When ready to cook, drain the meat, scraping off most of the marinade with a rubber spatula. (Scraping off the marinade will help the steak to sear better and makes less of a mess on the grill.) Drizzle the remaining 1 tablespoon of oil over the beef on both sides, spreading it over the meat with your fingertips.
5.   Turn control knob to the high position, butter the grill surface, when the griddle is hot, place the beef. A thick slab of sirloin or round steak will be cooked to medium-rare after 7 to 10 Minutes; flank steak will be cooked to medium after 3 to 5 Minutes.

6. To test for doneness, use the poke method; when cooked to medium-rare the meat should be gently yielding.

7. Transfer the meat to a cutting board and let rest for 3 Minutes. To serve, thinly slice the meat against the grain on a sharp diagonal. Fan out the slices on a platter or plate and serve at once.

Spare Ribs With Sweet Ancho-cumin Rub

Servings: 6
Cooking Time: 120 Minutes
Ingredients:
- 1 tablespoon sugar
- 2 teaspoons salt
- 2 teaspoons black pepper
- 2 teaspoons ground cumin
- 2 teaspoons ancho chile powder
- 2 teaspoons paprika
- About 4 pounds spare ribs

Directions:
1. Preparing the Ingredients
2. To make the rub, stir the sugar, salt, pepper, cumin, ancho powder, and paprika together in a small bowl. Rub into the ribs on both sides. (You can do this up to several hours ahead of cooking.)
3. Bring the griddle grill to medium heat. When the griddle is hot, put the ribs, meaty side up in the and cook for 120 Minutes.
4. Every half hour, turn. Cook until the meat is tender enough that you can easily cut between the ribs, 2 hours total.,
5. Transfer to a cutting board and let rest until cool enough to handle, then cut between the ribs, put on a platter, and serve.

Yucatan-style Grilled Pork

Servings: 4

Cooking Time: 8 Minutes
Ingredients:
- 2 pork tenderloins, trimmed
- 1 teaspoon annatto powder
- Olive oil
- For the marinade:
- 2 oranges, juiced
- 2 lemons, juiced, or more to taste
- 2 limes, juiced, or more to taste
- 6 cloves garlic, minced
- 1 teaspoon ground cumin
- 1/2 teaspoon cayenne pepper
- 1/2 teaspoon dried oregano
- 1/2 teaspoon black pepper

Directions:
1. Combine marinade ingredients in a mixing bowl and whisk until well-blended.
2. Cut the tenderloins in half crosswise; cut each piece in half lengthwise.
3. Place pieces in marinade and thoroughly coat with the mixture.
4. Cover with plastic wrap and refrigerate 4 to 6 hours.
5. Transfer pieces of pork from marinade to a paper-towel-lined bowl to absorb most of the moisture.
6. Discard paper towels. Drizzle olive oil and a bit more annatto powder on the pork.
7. Preheat griddle for medium-high heat and lightly oil.
8. Place pieces evenly spaced on griddle; cook 4 to 5 minutes.
9. Turn and cook on the other side another 4 or 5 minutes.
10. Transfer onto a serving platter and allow meat to rest about 5 minutes before serving.
Nutrition Info: Calories: 439, Sodium: 1382 mg, Dietary Fiber: 1.5g, Fat: 33.1g, Carbs:11.4g Protein: 23.9g

FISH & SEAFOOD RECIPES

Grilled Popcorn Shrimp

Servings: 5
Cooking Time: 3 Minutes
Ingredients:
- SPICERUB
- 2 teaspoons garlic powder
- 2 teaspoons sweet paprika
- 1 teaspoon onion powder
- 1 teaspoon dried oregano
- 1 teaspoon cayenne pepper
- 1 teaspoon salt
- 1 teaspoon freshly ground black pepper
- 1 teaspoon sugar
- In a large resealable plastic bag, combine the spices and shake to blend them. (The spice mix can be made ahead and kept nearly indefinitely.)
- SHRIMP
- 1½ pounds shelled and deveined small shrimp
- 1 lemon, cut into wedges

Directions:
1. Preparing the Ingredients
2. Add the shrimp to the plastic bag with the spice rub and shake to coat.
3. Turn control knob to the high position. Oil the griddle and allow it to heat until the oil is shimmering but not smoking. Grill the shrimp for about 1 minute per side, until they are opaque and firm to the touch.
4. Serve the shrimp immediately in a bowl garnished with the lemon wedges (and with plenty of napkins).
Nutrition Info: (Per Serving): CALORIES: 193; FAT52G; PROTEIN:35G

Halibut Fillets With Spinach And Olives

Servings: 4
Cooking Time: 10 Minutes
Ingredients:
- 4 (6 ounce) halibut fillets
- 1/3 cup olive oil
- 4 cups baby spinach
- 1/4 cup lemon juice
- 2 ounces pitted black olives, halved
- 2 tablespoons flat leaf parsley, chopped
- 2 teaspoons fresh dill, chopped
- Lemon wedges, to serve

Directions:
1. Preheat griddle to medium heat.
2. Toss spinach with lemon juice in a mixing bowl and set aside.
3. Brush fish with olive oil and cook for 3-4 minutes per side, or until cooked through.
4. Remove from heat, cover with foil and let rest for 5 minutes.
5. Add remaining oil and cook spinach for 2 minutes, or until just wilted. Remove from heat.
6. Toss with olives and herbs, then transfer to serving plates with fish, and serve with lemon wedges.
Nutrition Info: Calories: 773, Sodium: 1112 mg, Dietary Fiber: 1.4g, Fat: 36.6g, Carbs: 2.9g Protein: 109.3g

Lobster With Drawn Butter

Servings: 4
Cooking Time: 10 Minutes
Ingredients:
- ½ pound (2 sticks) butter
- 4 live lobsters (1¼ to 1½ pounds each)
- Salt and pepper
- 4 lemons, halved

Directions:
1. Preparing the Ingredients
2. 1 Melt the butter in a small saucepan over low heat until it foams. Remove the pan from the heat and skim away the foam. Let the pan sit for several Minutes for the milk solids to settle to the bottom. Ladle the clear yellow butterfat into a microwave-safe bowl. (You can clarify the butter up to a day ahead, cover, and refrigerate it.)
3. Bring a large pot of water to a boil and salt it. Fill the sink or a very large bowl with an ice bath.
4. Working in batches if your pot isn't large enough, put the lobsters in the boiling water with tongs. Cover the pot and cook until they turn bright red, about 2 Minutes depending on their size. (The water may not return to a boil.) Transfer the lobsters to the

ice bath to stop the cooking, then drain; add more ice and repeat the process with the remaining lobsters if necessary.

5.   Split the lobsters in half along the back with a sharp knife, in one fell swoop if you can. If you like, use a spoon to clean out the gills and anything that doesn't look like meat from the torso.

6.   2 Bring the griddle grill to high heat. Oil the griddle. Put the lobsters shell side down on the griddle. Cook, checking every couple of Minutes and turning once, until they're firm and just opaque at the center, 3 to 5 Minutes a side. When you turn the lobsters, put the lemon halves on the grate, cut side down.

7.   3 Heap the lobsters onto a serving platter. Reheat the butter in the microwave, and serve each lobster with a lemon half and a small bowl of drawn butter for dipping.

Mussels With Pancetta Aïoli

Servings: 4
Cooking Time: 5 Minutes
Ingredients:

- ¾ cup mayonnaise
- 1 tablespoon minced garlic, or more to taste
- 1 4-ounce slice pancetta, chopped
- Salt and pepper
- 4 pounds mussels
- 8 thick slices Italian bread
- ¼ cup good-quality olive oil

Directions:

1.   Preparing the Ingredients

2.   1 Whisk the mayonnaise and garlic together in a small bowl. Put the pancetta in a cold small skillet and turn the heat to low; cook, stirring occasionally, until most of the fat is rendered and the meat turns golden and crisp, about 5 Minutes. Drain on a paper towel, then stir into the mayonnaise along with 1 teaspoon of the rendered fat from the pan. Taste and add more garlic and some salt if you like. Cover and refrigerate until you're ready to serve. (You can make the aïoli up to several days ahead; refrigerate in an airtight container.)

3.   Rinse the mussels and pull off any beards. Discard any that are broken or don't close when tapped.

4.   Brush both sides of the bread slices with the oil.

5.   Bring the griddle grill to high heat. Oil the griddle. Put the bread on the grill and toast, turning once, until it develops grill marks with some charring, 1 to 2 Minutes per side. Remove from the grill and keep warm.

6.   Scatter the mussels onto the griddle, spreading them out so they are in a single layer. Cook for 3 Minutes. Transfer the open mussels to a large bowl with tongs. If any have not opened, leave them on the grill, and cook for another minute or 2, checking frequently and removing open mussels until they are all off the grill.

7.   2 Dollop the aïoli over the tops of the mussels and use a large spoon to turn the mussels over to coat them. Serve the mussels drizzled with their juices, either over (or alongside) the bread.

Salmon Zucchini Patties

Servings: 6
Cooking Time: 10 Minutes
Ingredients:

- 2 eggs
- 1 1/2 lbs salmon, cooked
- 2 cups zucchini, shredded
- 2 tbsp onion, minced
- 1/4 cup fresh cilantro, chopped
- 1/4 cup olive oil
- 3/4 cup almond flour
- 3 tbsp fresh lime juice
- 2 tbsp jalapeno, minced
- 2 tsp salt

Directions:

1.   Add salmon, lime juice, cilantro, zucchini, jalapenos, onion, eggs, and salt into the food processor and process until the mixture is combined.

2.   Add almond flour to a shallow dish.

3.   Preheat the griddle to high heat. Add oil to griddle.

4.   Take 1/4 cup salmon mixture and form patties, coat patties with almond flour then place onto the hot griddle top and cook for 5 minutes per side.

5.   Serve and enjoy.

Nutrition Info: (Per Serving): Calories 330 ;Fat 24 g ;Carbohydrates 5 g ;Sugar 1.5 g ;Protein 27.4 g ;Cholesterol 105 mg

Hibachi Salmon

Servings: 4
Cooking Time: 10 Minutes
Ingredients:

- 2 lbs. salmon fillets
- 1/2 cup teriyaki sauce
- 1 tsp. fresh grated ginger
- 2 cloves garlic
- 1/4 cup brown sugar
- 2 tsp. black pepper
- 1 Tbsp. maple syrup

Directions:

1.   Mix all the ingredients together in a covered glass bowl or resealable bag, and refrigerate for several hours to overnight.

2.   Heat the griddle grill to high, and grill the salmon fillets for 3–4 minutes per side until cooked through. Salmon should be homogeneous in color with white juice between the flakes.

3.   Let rest for several minutes before serving.

Nutrition Info: (Per serving):Calories 251, Carbs, 3g, Fat 13g, Protein 30g

Spicy Grilled Squid

Servings: 4
Cooking Time: 5 Minutes
Ingredients:

- 1 ½ lbs. Squid, prepared
- Olive oil
- For the marinade:
- 2 cloves garlic cloves, minced
- ½ teaspoon ginger, minced
- 3 tablespoons gochujang
- 3 tablespoons corn syrup
- 1 teaspoon yellow mustard
- 1 teaspoon soy sauce
- 2 teaspoons sesame oil
- 1 teaspoon sesame seeds

- 2 green onions, chopped

Directions:

1.   Preheat griddle to medium high heat and brush with olive oil.

2.   Add the squid and tentacles to the griddle and cook for 1 minute until the bottom looks firm and opaque.

3.   Turn them over and cook for another minute; straighten out the body with tongs if it curls.

4.   Baste with sauce on top of the squid and cook 2 additional minutes.

5.   Flip and baste the other side, cook 1 minute until the sauce evaporates and the squid turns red and shiny.

Nutrition Info: Calories: 292, Sodium: 466 mg, Dietary Fiber: 2.7g, Fat: 8.6g, Carbs: 25.1g Protein: 27.8g

Tuna With Fresh Tomato-basil Sauce

Servings: 4
Cooking Time: 20 Minutes
Ingredients:

- TOMATO-BASIL SAUCE
- 2 tablespoons olive oil
- 1 small yellow onion, diced
- ¼ teaspoon salt
- ½ pint cherry tomatoes, cut in half
- 2 tablespoons water
- ¼ cup fresh basil leaves, chopped
- TUNA
- 1 tablespoon olive oil
- 4 (6-ounce) tuna steaks, about 1 inch thick

Directions:

1.   Preparing the Ingredients

2.   In a medium saucepan, heat the olive oil over medium heat. Add the onion and salt. Cook, stirring frequently, until the onion is golden brown, 10 to 15 Minutes. Add the tomatoes and water and cook for approximately 5 to 7 Minutes, until the tomatoes have softened and wrinkled. (The sauce can be cooled, covered, and refrigerated overnight. Reheat before serving.) Stir in the basil just before serving.

3.   Bring the griddle grill to high heat. Oil the griddle. Rub the olive oil over the tuna steaks. Grill for about 4 Minutes. To test for doneness, prod on

edge of the tuna with a fork. The fish should flake, but the center will still be a bit rosy.

4.   Spoon the tuna into 4 shallow bowls and top with the warm tomato-basil sauce.

Nutrition Info: (Per Serving): CALORIES: 289; FAT:12G; PROTEIN:40G; SUGAR:4G

Whole Fish With Basil-orange Oil

Servings: 4

Cooking Time: 16 Minutes

Ingredients:

- ¼ cup good-quality olive oil, plus more for brushing the fish
- 2 cloves garlic, thinly sliced
- 1 orange
- 2 1½-pound or 4 12- to 16-ounce whole fish, scaled and gutted
- Salt and pepper
- 8–12 large sprigs fresh basil
- 2 tablespoons chopped fresh basil

Directions:

1.   Preparing the Ingredients

2.   Put the oil and garlic in a small saucepan or skillet over the lowest heat possible. When the garlic begins to sizzle, swirl the oil a bit, then turn the heat off; don't allow the garlic to brown.

3.   Grate 2 teaspoons zest from the rind of the orange, then slice the orange thinly, removing any seeds.

4.   Pat the fish dry with paper towels. Brush them on both sides with olive oil and sprinkle with salt and pepper on both sides and in the cavity. Divide the orange slices between the fish, overlapping them in the cavities. Put the basil sprigs on top of the orange slices and close the fish.

5.   Turn control knob to the high position. Oil the griddle and allow it to heat. Put the fish on the griddle and cook until the skin browns and the fish release easily, 10 to 12 Minutes. Carefully turn the fish, using a second spatula to lower them back down to the grate and cook until a skewer or thin knife inserted at the thickest point easily pierces it all the way through, 4 to 6 Minutes. Transfer the fish to a platter.

6.   Heat the oil and garlic over low heat. When the garlic begins to sizzle, stir in the orange zest and chopped basil and remove from the heat.

7.   Remove the fillets from both sides of the fish by cutting horizontally between the flesh and the bones with a sharp knife and a spatula. Try to keep them intact, and remove as many bones as possible. Drizzle the warm orange-basil oil over the fillets and serve the carcass alongside if you like.

Blackened Tilapia

Servings: 4

Cooking Time: 6 Minutes

Ingredients:

- 4 tilapia fillets
- 2 tbsp butter
- 1 tbsp olive oil
- For seasoning:
- 1 1/2 tsp paprika
- 1 lemon, sliced
- 1/2 tsp ground cumin
- 1 tsp oregano
- 1/2 tsp garlic powder
- Pepper
- Salt

Directions:

1.   In a small bowl, mix together all seasoning ingredients and rub over fish fillets.

2.   Preheat the griddle to high heat.

3.   Add butter and oil on the hot griddle top.

4.   Place fish fillets onto the griddle top and cook for 3 minutes.

5.   Turn fish fillets and cook for 3 minutes more or until cooked through.

6.   Serve and enjoy.

Nutrition Info: (Per Serving): Calories 181 ;Fat 10.5 g ;Carbohydrates 1.2 g ;Sugar 0.2 g ;Protein 21.4 g ;Cholesterol 70 mg

Grilled Salmon With A Mustard And Brown Sugar Crust

Servings: 4

Cooking Time: 5 Minutes

Ingredients:

- 4pieces salmon fillet (each about 6 ounces)
- Coarse salt (kosher or sea) and freshly ground black pepper
- 1 cup firmly packed dark brown sugar
- 3 tablespoons Dijon mustard
- Sweet Mustard and Dill Sauce
- SWEETMUSTARD AND DILL SAUCE
- ⅓cup mayonnaise(preferably Hellmann's)
- ⅓ cup sour cream
- ⅓ cup Dijon or Meaux mustard
- 2 tablespoons chopped fresh dill
- 1 tablespoon brown sugar (dark or light), or more to taste
- Freshly ground black pepper

Directions:

1. Preparing the Ingredients
2. Place the mayonnaise, sour cream, mustard, dill, and brown sugar in a small nonreactive bowl and whisk to mix. Taste for seasoning, adding more brown sugar and pepper to taste. The sauce can be refrigerated, covered, for several days.
3. Run your fingers over the salmon fillets, feeling for bones. Using needle-nose pliers or tweezers, pull out any you find. Rinse the fish under cold running water, then blot it dry with paper towels. Very generously season the salmon on both sides with salt and pepper.
4. Spread the brown sugar out in a large shallow bowl, crumbling it between your fingers or with a fork. Brush or spread each salmon fillet on both sides with the mustard. Dredge both sides of each fillet in the brown sugar, patting it onto the fish with your fingertips. Gently shake off any excess brown sugar; the fish should be fairly thickly crusted.
5. Turn control knob to the high position. Oil the griddle and allow it to heat. Arrange the salmon on the hot Griddle. The salmon will be done after cooking 3 to 5 Minutes until the outside is darkly browned and the fish is cooked through. To test for doneness, press the fish with your finger; it should break into clean flakes.
6. Transfer the salmon to a platter or plates and serve at once.

Seafood Stuffed Sole

Servings: 2
Cooking Time: 14 Minutes
Ingredients:

- 1/4 cup shrimp, cooked, peeled and chopped
- 1 tablespoon lemon juice
- 2 tablespoons butter, melted, divided
- 3/4 cup cherry tomatoes
- 1 tablespoon chicken broth
- 1/2 can (6-ounces) crabmeat, drained
- 1/2 teaspoon parsley, fresh minced
- 1 tablespoon whipped cream cheese
- 1/2 teaspoon grated lemon zest
- 2 tablespoons breadcrumbs
- 1 teaspoon chive, minced
- 2 (6-ounces) sole fish fillets, cut from the side with gutted and cleaned
- 1/4 teaspoon black ground pepper

Directions:

1. Mix your cream cheese, cram, shrimp, garlic, lemon zest, parsley, 2 tablespoons butter and breadcrumbs in a mixing bowl.
2. Stuff each fillet with 1/4 of this mixture and secure the ends with toothpicks.
3. Mix lemon juice, tomatoes, salt and pepper in a different bowl.
4. Place your stuffed fillets in a foil sheet and top with the tomato mixture.
5. Cover and seal the fillets in foil.
6. Preheat your griddle grill on the medium temperature setting.
7. Once your grill is preheated, place 2 sealed fillets on the grill.
8. Grill it for 7 minutes per side. Serve and Enjoy!

Nutrition Info: (Per serving): Calories: 248 Fat: 2.7g Carbs: 31.4g Protein: 24.9g

Octopus With Lemon And Oregano

Servings: 4
Cooking Time: 10 Minutes
Ingredients:

- 3 lemons
- 3 pounds cleaned octopus, thawed if frozen
- 6 cloves garlic, peeled
- 4 sprigs fresh oregano

- 2 bay leaves
- Salt and pepper
- 3 tablespoons good-quality olive oil
- Minced fresh oregano for garnish

Directions:
1. Preparing the Ingredients
2. 1 Halve one of the lemons. Put the octopus, garlic, oregano sprigs, bay leaves, a large pinch of salt, and lemon halves in a large pot with enough water to cover by a couple of inches. Bring to a boil, adjust the heat so the liquid bubbles gently but steadily, and cook, turning occasionally with tongs, until the octopus is tender, 30 to 90 Minutes. (Check with the tip of a sharp knife; it should go in easily.) Drain; discard the seasonings. (You can cover and refrigerate the octopus for up to 24 hours.)
3. Squeeze the juice 1 of the remaining lemons and whisk it with the oil and salt and pepper to taste. Cut the octopus into large serving pieces and toss with the oil mixture.
4. 2 Bring the griddle grill to high heat. Oil the griddle. Put the octopus on the grill, and cook until heated through and charred, 4 to 5 Minutes per side. Cut the remaining lemon in wedges. Transfer the octopus to a platter, sprinkle with minced oregano, and serve with the lemon wedges.

Pesto Shrimp

Servings: 4
Cooking Time: 5 Minutes
Ingredients:
- 1 lb shrimp, remove shells and tails
- 1/2 cup basil pesto
- Pepper
- Salt

Directions:
1. Add shrimp, pesto, pepper, and salt into the large bowl and toss well. Set aside for 15 minutes.
2. Heat grill over medium-high heat.
3. Thread marinated shrimp onto the skewers and place onto the hot griddle top and cook for 1-2 minutes on each side.
4. Serve and enjoy.

Nutrition Info: (Per Serving): Calories 270 ;Fat 15 g ;Carbohydrates 3.7 g ;Sugar 2 g ;Protein 28.8 g ;Cholesterol 246 mg

Healthy Salmon Patties

Servings: 2
Cooking Time: 10 Minutes
Ingredients:
- 6 oz can salmon, drained, remove bones, and pat dry
- 2 tbsp mayonnaise
- 1/2 cup almond flour
- 1/4 tsp thyme
- 1 egg, lightly beaten
- 2 tbsp olive oil
- Pepper
- Salt

Directions:
1. Add salmon, thyme, egg, mayonnaise, almond flour, pepper, and salt into the mixing bowl and mix until well combined.
2. Preheat the griddle to high heat.
3. Add oil to the griddle top.
4. Make small patties from salmon mixture and place onto the hot griddle top and cook for 5-6 minutes.
5. Turn patties and cook for 3-4 minutes more.
6. Serve and enjoy.

Nutrition Info: (Per Serving): Calories 530 ;Fat 41 g ;Carbohydrates 9.8 g ;Sugar 1.1 g ;Protein 30.6 g ;Cholesterol 146 mg

Tasty Shrimp Skewers

Servings: 6
Cooking Time: 7 Minutes
Ingredients:
- 1 1/2 lbs shrimp, peeled and deveined
- 1 tbsp dried oregano
- 2 tsp garlic paste
- 2 lemon juice
- 1/4 cup olive oil
- 1 tsp paprika
- Pepper
- Salt

Directions:
1. Add all ingredients into the mixing bowl and mix well and place in the refrigerator for 1 hour.
2. Remove marinated shrimp from refrigerator and thread onto the skewers.
3. Preheat the griddle to high heat.
4. Place skewers onto the griddle top and cook for 5-7 minutes.
5. Serve and enjoy.
Nutrition Info: (Per Serving): Calories 212 ;Fat 10.5 g ;Carbohydrates 2.7 g ;Sugar 0.1 g ;Protein 26 g ;Cholesterol 239 mg

Shrimp

Servings: 4
Cooking Time: 5 Minutes
Ingredients:
- Large Raw Shrimp, Peeled And Mud Vein Removed
- Olive Oil
- Garlic Salt To Taste
- Fresh Lime Juice

Directions:
1. Preheat the griddle grill to high.
2. Place the shrimp on the skewers through the center in the same direction.
3. Brush with olive oil and sprinkle with garlic salt.
4. Place the skewers on the grill and cook for 2 minutes on each side or until the half toward the heat has turned pink and white.
5. Drizzle with the lime juice, and grill a few seconds per side.
6. Remove from heat and serve immediately.
Nutrition Info: (Per serving):Calories 101, Fat 1.4g, carbs 6g, protein 10g

Spicy Lemon Butter Shrimp

Servings: 4
Cooking Time: 10 Minutes
Ingredients:
- 1 1/2 lbs shrimp, peeled and deveined
- 3 garlic cloves, minced
- 1 small onion, minced
- 1/2 cup butter

- 1 1/2 tbsp fresh parsley, chopped
- 1 tbsp fresh lemon juice
- 1/4 tsp red pepper flakes
- Pepper
- Salt

Directions:
1. Preheat the griddle to high heat.
2. Melt butter on the griddle top.
3. Add garlic, onion, red chili flakes, pepper, and salt and stir for 2 minutes.
4. Season shrimp with pepper and salt and thread onto skewers.
5. Brush shrimp skewers with butter mixture.
6. Place shrimp skewers on griddle top and cook until shrimp turns to pink, about 3-4 minutes.
7. Transfer shrimp to the serving plate.
8. Drizzle lemon juice over shrimp and garnish with parsley.
9. Serve and enjoy.
Nutrition Info: (Per Serving): Calories 419 ;Fat 25 g ;Carbohydrates 5.2 g ;Sugar 0.9 g ;Protein 39.4 g ;Cholesterol 419 mg

Seared Scallops With Parsley-lemon Stuffing

Servings: 4
Cooking Time: 10 Minutes
Ingredients:
- ½ cup minced fresh parsley
- 2 teaspoons grated lemon zest
- 1 clove garlic, minced
- Salt and pepper
- 1½ pounds sea scallops, trimmed of any tough connective tissue
- Good-quality olive oil for brushing the scallops
- Lemon wedges for serving

Directions:
1. Preparing the Ingredients
2. Stir the parsley, lemon zest, and garlic together in a small bowl and sprinkle with a little salt and pepper if you like.
3. Pat the scallops dry with paper towels. Brush them with oil and season with salt and pepper on both sides. With a small thin knife, make a 1-to 1½-inch-long horizontal slit in the side, going almost all

the way through. Jiggle the knife from side to side to enlarge the pocket without cutting through the side. Using a small spoon with a pointed tip, like a grapefruit spoon, fill each scallop with the stuffing. (You can prepare and refrigerate the scallops up to several hours in advance.)

4.   Bring the griddle grill to high heat. Oil the griddle. Put the scallops on the grill, and cook until they're seared and golden brown in spots, with the centers still ever so slightly translucent, 8 to 10 Minutes. Transfer the scallops to a platter and serve with lemon wedges.

Swordfish

Servings: 4
Cooking Time: 15 Minutes
Ingredients:
*   Swordfish Fillets, Cut About 1.5 Inches Thick
*   Olive Oil
*   Sea Salt And Pepper To Taste
Directions:
1.   Preheat the griddle grill to high.
2.   Drizzle the fillets with olive oil and season with sea salt and black pepper.
3.   Place on the grill and cook for 3 minutes per side.
4.   Turn the grill down to medium and continue grilling for 5 minutes per side or until the sides of the swordfish are homogeneous in color.
5.   Let the fish relax for 5 minutes before serving.
Nutrition Info: (Per serving): Calories: 132, carbs 8g, Protein: 22 g, Fat: 4 g

Salmon

Servings: 4
Cooking Time: 15 Minutes
Ingredients:
*   Boneless Salmon Fillets, Scaled
*   Olive Oil
*   Sea Salt And Pepper To Taste
Directions:
1.   Preheat the griddle grill to high.
2.   Drizzle the fillets with olive oil and season with sea salt and black pepper.

3.   Place on the griddle grill, and cook for 3 minutes per side.
4.   Turn the grill down to medium and continue grilling for several minutes until the fillet is homogeneous in color and white is beginning to appear on top of the fillet.
5.   Remove from heat, and let it rest for a few minutes before serving.
Nutrition Info: (Per serving):Calories 170kcal, Fat 8g, carbs 15g, Protein 26g

Grilled Teriyaki-glazed Coho Salmon

Servings: 2
Cooking Time: 25 Minutes
Ingredients:
*   1–2 coho salmon filets
*   SAUCE
*   1 cup water
*   ¼ cup brown sugar
*   ¼ cup soy sauce
*   1 Tbsp. honey
*   1½ Tbsp. finely minced ginger root (about 1-inch piece)
*   2 cloves garlic, finely minced
*   ½ tsp. white pepper
*   THICKENER
*   2 Tbsp. cornstarch
*   ¼ cup cold water
Directions:
1.   Preparing the Ingredients
2.   In medium saucepan over medium heat, combine sauce ingredients and bring to a low boil.
3.   Once sauce reaches a low boil, use a fork and mix together cornstarch and water in separate bowl until thoroughly incorporated. Slowly whisk cornstarch mixture into sauce until it thickens.
4.   Add one chunk of pecan wood to the hot coals of your grill
5.   Brush sauce onto salmon filets.
6.   Bring the griddle grill to high heat. Oil the griddle, and cook for 15 Minutes.
7.   Brush salmon with another coat of sauce, and cook for an additional 10 Minutes.
8.   Remove from grill, garnish, and serve hot.

Garlic Butter Tilapia

Servings: 6
Cooking Time: 8 Minutes
Ingredients:
- 2 lbs tilapia fillets
- 1 tsp garlic powder
- 1/2 fresh lemon juice
- 1 tbsp butter, melted
- Pepper
- Salt

Directions:
1. In a small bowl, combine together lemon juice, garlic powder, and butter and microwave for 10 seconds.
2. Brush both the side of the fish fillet with lemon mixture. Season fillet with pepper and salt.
3. Preheat the griddle to high heat.
4. Spray griddle top with cooking spray.
5. Place fillets on hot griddle top and cook for 4 minutes on each side.
6. Serve and enjoy.
Nutrition Info: (Per Serving): Calories 143 ;Fat 3 g ;Carbohydrates 0.4 g ;Sugar 0.1 g ;Protein 28.2 g ;Cholesterol 79 mg

Blackened Salmon

Servings: 5
Cooking Time: 10 Minutes
Ingredients:
- 1 1/4 lbs salmon fillets
- 2 tbsp blackened seasoning
- 2 tbsp butter

Directions:
1. Season salmon fillets with blackened seasoning.
2. Preheat the griddle to high heat.
3. Melt butter on the griddle top.
4. Place salmon fillets onto the hot griddle top and cook for 4-5 minutes.
5. Turn salmon and cook for 4-5 minutes more.
6. Serve and enjoy.
Nutrition Info: (Per Serving): Calories 190 ;Fat 11 g ;Carbohydrates 0 g ;Sugar 0 g ;Protein 21.1 g ;Cholesterol 62 mg

Flavorful Mexican Shrimp

Servings: 4
Cooking Time: 12 Minutes
Ingredients:
- 1 lb shrimp, cleaned
- 3 tbsp fresh parsley, chopped
- 1 tbsp garlic, minced
- 1/4 onion, sliced
- 1/4 tsp paprika
- 1/4 tsp ground cumin
- 2 fresh lime juice
- 2 tbsp olive oil
- 1/4 cup butter
- Pepper
- Salt

Directions:
1. Season shrimp with paprika, cumin, pepper, and salt.
2. Preheat the griddle to high heat.
3. Add oil and butter to the griddle top.
4. Add onion and garlic and sauté for 5 minutes.
5. Add shrimp and cook for 5-8 minutes or until cooked.
6. Add parsley and lime juice.
7. Stir well and serve.
Nutrition Info: (Per Serving): Calories 311 ;Fat 20.5 g ;Carbohydrates 5 g ;Sugar 0.7 g ;Protein 26.4 g ;Cholesterol 269 mg

Lime Ginger Salmon

Servings: 5
Cooking Time: 10 Minutes
Ingredients:
- 1 teaspoon onion, finely chopped
- 1/4 teaspoon sea salt
- 1 teaspoon ginger root, fresh minced
- 1 tablespoon rice vinegar
- 1 garlic clove, minced
- 2 teaspoons sugar
- 1/8 cup lime juice
- 1 cucumber, peeled and chopped
- 1/6 cup cilantro, fresh chopped
- 1/4 teaspoon coriander, ground
- 1/4 teaspoon ground pepper

- Salmon:
- 5 (6-ounces) salmon fillets
- 1/4 teaspoon of sea salt
- 1/4 teaspoon freshly ground black pepper
- 1/6 cup ginger root, minced
- 1/2 tablespoon olive oil
- 1/2 tablespoon lime juice

Directions:
1. Begin by blending the first 11 ingredients in a blender until smooth.
2. Season your salmon fillets with olive oil, lime juice, ginger, salt and pepper.
3. Preheat your griddle grill to the medium temperature setting.
4. Once your grill is preheated, place 2 salmon fillets on the grill.
5. Grill it for 4 minutes per side.
6. Cook the remaining fillets in the same manner.
7. Serve salmon fillets with prepared sauce and enjoy!

Nutrition Info: (Per serving): Calories: 457 Fat: 19.1g Carbs; 18.9g Protein: 32.5g

Sardines With Lemon And Thyme

Servings: 2
Cooking Time: 8 Minutes
Ingredients:

- 1 pound fresh sardines, cleaned
- Good-quality olive oil for brushing the fish
- Salt and pepper
- 1 small bunch fresh thyme
- Lemon wedges for serving

Directions:
1. Preparing the Ingredients
2. Brush the fish with oil and season with salt and pepper on both sides and in the cavity. Tuck in the thyme sprigs.
3. Bring the griddle grill to high heat. Oil the griddle and allow it to heat. Put the fish and cook until the skin is charred in places and the fish release easily, 8 Minutes. Transfer the fish to a platter and serve with lemon wedges and a final sprinkle of salt.

Grilled Oysters With Spiced Tequila Butter

Servings: 6
Cooking Time: 25 Minutes
Ingredients:

- 3 dozen medium oysters, scrubbed and shucked
- Flakey sea salt, for serving
- For the butter:
- 1/4 teaspoon crushed red pepper
- 7 tablespoons unsalted butter
- ¼ teaspoon chili oil
- 1 teaspoon dried oregano
- 2 tablespoons freshly squeezed lemon juice
- 2 tablespoons tequila blanco, like Espolon

Directions:
1. Combine butter ingredients in a small mixing bowl until well-incorporated and set aside.
2. Preheat griddle to high.
3. Grill the oysters about 1 to 2 minutes.
4. Sprinkle the oysters with salt flakes.
5. Warm the butter in a microwave for 30 seconds, and spoon the warm tequila butter over the oysters and serve.

Nutrition Info: Calories: 184, Sodium: 300 mg, Dietary Fiber: 0.2g, Fat: 15g, Carbs: 3.8g Protein: 0.2g

Rosemary Salmon

Servings: 4
Cooking Time: 5 Minutes
Ingredients:

- 4 rosemary branches
- 4 pieces skinless salmon fillet (each about 2 inches wide, 3 to 4 inches long, ¾ to 1 inch thick, and 6 ounces)
- 2 tablespoons extra-virgin olive oil
- Coarse salt (kosher or sea) and freshly ground black pepper
- 2 cloves garlic, minced
- 1 teaspoon finely grated lemon zest
- Lemon wedges, for serving

Directions:
1. Preparing the Ingredients
2. Strip the leaves off the bottom 4 inches of each rosemary branch (pull them off between your thumb and forefinger) and very finely chop the leaves; you'll use the chopped rosemary to season the salmon. Run your fingers over the salmon fillets, feeling for bones.

Using needle-nose pliers or tweezers, pull out any you find. Rinse the fish under cold running water, then blot it dry with paper towels. Skewer each salmon fillet on the bare part of a rosemary branch through the center of a short side. Place the fish on a large plate and brush on both sides with the olive oil. Generously season the fish on both sides with salt and pepper.

3.   Place the chopped rosemary and the garlic and lemon zest in a small bowl and stir to mix. Sprinkle the rosemary mixture over the salmon on all sides, patting it onto the fish with your fingertips. Let the fish stand at room temperature while you preheat the grill.

4.   Bring the griddle grill to high heat. Oil the griddle and allow it to heat. Arrange the salmon on the hot grill. It will be done after cooking 3 to 5 Minutes. To test for doneness, press the fish with your finger; it should break into clean flakes.

5.   Transfer the salmon to a platter or plates and serve it with lemon wedges on the side.

Moroccan Salmon

Servings: 4
Cooking Time: 5 Minutes
Ingredients:
- ½ cup fresh cilantro leaves
- ½ cup fresh flat-leaf parsley leaves
- 2 cloves garlic, coarsely chopped
- 1 teaspoon sweet paprika
- ½ teaspoon coarse salt (kosher or sea), or more to taste
- ½ teaspoon freshly ground black pepper
- ½ teaspoon ground coriander
- ½ teaspoon ground cumin
- ½ teaspoon hot red pepper flakes, or more to taste
- 3 tablespoons fresh lemon juice, or more to taste
- ½ cup extra-virgin olive oil
- 4 pieces salmon fillet or salmon steaks (each 6 to 8 ounces)

Directions:
1.   Preparing the Ingredients
2.   Place the cilantro, parsley, garlic, paprika, salt, black pepper, coriander, cumin, and hot pepper flakes in a food processor and pulse the machine to finely chop. Add the lemon juice and process until a coarse purée forms. With the motor running, add the olive oil in a thin stream. Taste for seasoning, adding more salt, hot pepper flakes, and/or lemon juice as necessary; the charmoula should be highly seasoned.

3.   If using salmon fillets, run your fingers over them, feeling for bones. Using needle-nose pliers or tweezers, pull out any you find (you will not need to do this with salmon steaks). Rinse the fish under cold running water, then blot it dry with paper towels. Pour a third of the charmoula over the bottom of a nonreactive baking dish just large enough to hold the salmon in one layer. Arrange the salmon pieces on top. Spoon half of the remaining charmoula over the fish, then set the rest of the charmoula aside. Let the salmon marinate in the refrigerator, covered, for 2 to 4 hours (the longer it marinates, the richer the flavor will be).

4.   When ready to cook, drain the salmon and discard the marinade.

5.   Bring the griddle grill to high heat. Oil the griddle, when is hot, place the salmon. The salmon will be done after cooking 3 to 5 Minutes until it is browned and cooked through. To test for doneness, press the fish with your finger; it should break into clean flakes.

6.   Arrange the salmon on a platter or plates. Stir the remaining charmoula to recombine, then spoon it on top of the salmon.

Scallops

Servings: 4
Cooking Time: 10 Minutes
Ingredients:
- Large Fresh Bay Scallops
- Real Butter, Melted
- Sea Salt And Pepper To Taste

Directions:
1.   Preheat the griddle grill to high.
2.   Melt the butter, and set it aside so that it is ready for later.
3.   Season the scallops with salt and pepper.
4.   Spray the grill with spray oil, and immediately place the scallops on the heat. Brush the tops with butter.
5.   Grill for 3–4 minutes per side, brushing with the butter again after flipping. The scallops are ready to turn when they pull away easily from the grill.

6.	Brush the scallops again with the butter, and grill for an additional thirty seconds per side.
7.	Let the scallops relax for 5 minutes before serving.
Nutrition Info: (Per serving):Calories 1070, Carbs 240g, Fat 89g, Protein 77g

Lobster Tails With Lime Basil Butter

Servings: 4
Cooking Time: 6 Minutes
Ingredients:
- 4 lobster tails (cut in half lengthwise)
- 3 tablespoons olive oil
- lime wedges (to serve)
- Sea salt, to taste
- For the lime basil butter:
- 1 stick unsalted butter, softened
- 1/2 bunch basil, roughly chopped
- 1 lime, zested and juiced
- 2 cloves garlic, minced
- 1/4 teaspoon red pepper flakes

Directions:
1.	Add the butter ingredients to a mixing bowl and combine; set aside until ready to use.
2.	Preheat griddle to medium-high heat.
3.	Drizzle the lobster tail halves with olive oil and season with salt and pepper.
4.	Place the lobster tails, flesh-side down, on the griddle.
5.	Allow to cook until opaque, about 3 minutes, flip and cook another 3 minutes.
6.	Add a dollop of the lime basil butter during the last minute of cooking.
7.	Serve immediately.
Nutrition Info: Calories: 430, Sodium: 926 mg, Dietary Fiber: 0.5g, Fat: 34.7g, Carbs: 2.4g Protein: 28g

Paprika Garlic Shrimp

Servings: 4
Cooking Time: 5 Minutes
Ingredients:
- 1 lb shrimp, peeled and cleaned
- 5 garlic cloves, chopped
- 2 tbsp olive oil
- 1 tbsp fresh parsley, chopped
- 1 tsp paprika
- 2 tbsp butter
- 1/2 tsp sea salt

Directions:
1.	Add shrimp, 1 tbsp oil, garlic, and salt in a large bowl and toss well and place in the refrigerator for 1 hour.
2.	Preheat the griddle to high heat.
3.	Add remaining oil and butter on the hot griddle top.
4.	Once butter is melted then add marinated shrimp and paprika and stir constantly for 2-3 minutes or until shrimp is cooked.
5.	Garnish with parsley and serve.
Nutrition Info: (Per Serving): Calories 253 ;Fat 15 g ;Carbohydrates 3.3 g ;Sugar 0.1 g ;Protein 26.2 g ;Cholesterol 254 mg

Summer Shrimp Salad

Servings: 5
Cooking Time: 3 Minutes
Ingredients:
- ½ pint cherry tomatoes
- 3 tablespoons olive oil
- ½ teaspoon salt
- 1 pound medium to thin asparagus, woody stems snapped off and discarded
- 1 pound shelled and deveined medium shrimp
- ¼ teaspoon freshly ground black pepper
- ¼ teaspoon dried thyme
- Grated zest and juice of ½ lemon

Directions:
1.	Preparing the Ingredients
2.	Quarter the cherry tomatoes and put them in a medium bowl. Add 1 tablespoon of the olive oil and ¼ teaspoon of the salt. Toss gently and set aside.
3.	In a medium bowl, pour 1 tablespoon of the olive oil over the asparagus spears and rub gently to coat them.
4.	Turn control knob to the high position. Oil the griddle and allow it to heat until the oil is shimmering but not smoking. Grill the asparagus for about 5 Minutes. The thicker ones will still have a bit of crunch to them and the thinner ones will be tender. Transfer to a cutting board; keep the griddle on high. When they are cool enough to handle, cut the spears into 1-inch pieces. Add to the cherry tomatoes.

5. Rinse the shrimp and pat dry with paper towels. Put them in a medium bowl, add the remaining tablespoon olive oil, and toss to coat. Grill the shrimp for about 3 Minutes, until they are opaque and firm to the touch.

6. Add the shrimp to the tomatoes and asparagus. Add the remaining ¼ teaspoon salt, the pepper, thyme, and lemon juice and zest, and toss to combine. Serve warm or at room temperature, or refrigerate and serve chilled.

Nutrition Info: (Per Serving): CALORIES: 240; FAT:13G; PROTEIN:25G

Coconut Pineapple Shrimp Skewers

Servings: 4
Cooking Time: 5 Minutes
Ingredients:

- 1-1/2 pounds uncooked jumbo shrimp, peeled and deveined
- 1/2 cup light coconut milk
- 1 tablespoon cilantro, chopped
- 4 teaspoons Tabasco Original Red Sauce
- 2 teaspoons soy sauce
- 1/4 cup freshly squeezed orange juice
- 1/4 cup freshly squeezed lime juice (from about 2 large limes)
- 3/4 pound pineapple, cut into 1 inch chunks
- Olive oil, for grilling

Directions:

1. Combine the coconut milk, cilantro, Tabasco sauce, soy sauce, orange juice, lime juice. Add the shrimp and toss to coat.

2. Cover and place in the refrigerator to marinate for 1 hour.

3. Thread shrimp and pineapple onto metal skewers, alternating each.

4. Preheat griddle to medium heat.

5. Cook 5-6 minutes, flipping once, until shrimp turn opaque pink.

6. Serve immediately.

Nutrition Info: Calories: 150, Sodium: 190 mg, Dietary Fiber: 1.9g, Fat: 10.8g, Carbs: 14.9g Protein: 1.5g

Salmon Skewers

Servings: 4
Cooking Time: 10 Minutes
Ingredients:

- 1 lb salmon fillets, cut into 1-inch cubes
- 2 tbsp soy sauce
- 1 tbsp toasted sesame seeds
- 1 lime zest
- 2 tsp olive oil
- 1 1/2 tbsp maple syrup
- 1 tsp ginger, crushed
- 1 lime juice

Directions:

1. In a bowl, mix together olive oil, soy sauce, lime zest, lime juice, maple syrup, and ginger.

2. Add salmon and stir to coat. Set aside for 10 minutes.

3. Preheat the griddle to high heat.

4. Slide marinated salmon pieces onto the skewers and cook on a hot griddle top for 8-10 minutes or until cooked through.

5. Sprinkle salmon skewers with sesame seeds and serve.

Nutrition Info: (Per Serving): Calories 209 ;Fat 10 g ;Carbohydrates 6.5 g ;Sugar 4.6 g ;Protein 22.9 g ;Cholesterol 50 mg

Bacon Wrapped Scallops

Servings: 4
Cooking Time: 4 Minutes
Ingredients:

- 12 large sea scallops, side muscle removed
- 8 slices of bacon
- 1 tablespoon vegetable oil
- 12 toothpicks

Directions:

1. Heat your griddle to medium heat and cook the bacon until fat has rendered but bacon is still flexible. Remove bacon from the griddle and place on paper towels.

2. Raise griddle heat to medium-high.

3. Wrap each scallop with a half slice of bacon and skewer with a toothpick to keep the bacon in place.

4. Place the scallops on the griddle and cook for 90 seconds per side. They should be lightly browned on both sides.

5. Remove from the griddle and serve immediately.

Nutrition Info: Calories: 315, Sodium: 1023 mg, Dietary Fiber: 0g, Fat: 20g, Carbs:2.7g Protein: 29.2g

"barbecued" Salmon

Servings: 4
Cooking Time: 5 Minutes
Ingredients:
- 4 pieces skinless salmon fillet (each about 6 ounces)
- 2 tablespoons Basic Barbecue Rub
- 2 tablespoons olive oil
- 1 teaspoon liquid smoke
- BARBECUE VINAIGRETTE
- 1 tablespoon red barbecue sauce
- 1 tablespoon fresh lemon juice
- 3 tablespoons olive oil
- 1 tablespoon very finely diced sweet onion
- 1 tablespoon very finely diced seeded tomato
- 1 tablespoon very finely diced green bell pepper
- Coarse salt (kosher or sea) and freshly ground black pepper

Directions:
1. Preparing the Ingredients
2. Run your fingers over the fish fillets, feeling for bones. Using needle-nose pliers or tweezers, pull out any you find. Rinse the fish under cold running water, then blot it dry with paper towels. Sprinkle the barbecue rub all over the fish, patting it on with your fingertips. Let the fish cure at room temperature for 10 Minutes.
3. Place the olive oil and liquid smoke in a small bowl and stir with a fork. Set the basting mixture aside.
4. Bring the griddle grill to high heat. Oil the griddle. Place the fish on the hot griddle grill. The fish will be cooked through after 3 to 5 Minutes (if you prefer it pink in the center, cook it a minute or so less). You will need to turn the fish so that you can baste both sides until it is just cooked through. To test for doneness, press the fish with your finger; it should break into clean flakes. Start basting the fish with the olive oil mixture after 1 minute and baste both sides at least twice.
5. Transfer the fish to a platter or plates. Spoon the Barbecue Vinaigrette on top, if using, and serve at once.
6. BARBECUE VINAIGRETTE
7. Place the barbecue sauce in a small nonreactive bowl. Gradually whisk in 2 tablespoons of water and the lemon juice, olive oil, onion, tomato, and bell pepper. Season with salt and pepper to taste. The sauce is best made no more than an hour before serving.

Pesto Pistachio Shrimp

Servings: 4
Cooking Time: 10 Minutes
Ingredients:
- 1-1/2 lb. Uncooked shrimp, peeled and deveined
- 2 tablespoons lemon juice
- 1/4 cup Parmesan cheese, shredded
- 1/4 teaspoon of sea salt
- 1/8 teaspoon black ground pepper
- 1/2 cup olive oil
- 1/2 cup parsley, fresh minced
- 1 garlic clove, peeled
- 1/3 cup pistachios, shelled
- 1/4 teaspoon grated lemon zest
- 3/4 cup arugula, fresh

Directions:
1. Begin by adding the olive oil, lemon zest, garlic clove, pistachios, parsley, arugula and lemon juice to a blender. Blend until smooth.
2. Add your Parmesan cheese, sea salt and pepper, then mix well.
3. Toss in your shrimp and allow to marinate in the fridge for 30 minutes.
4. Thread your shrimp onto skewers.
5. Preheat your griddle grill on the medium temperature setting.
6. Once preheated, add your skewers onto the grill and close lid.
7. Grill for 6 minutes. Rotate the skewers every 2 minutes. Cooking skewers in batches. Serve and enjoy!

Nutrition Info: (Per serving): Calories: 293, Fat: 16g, Carbs: 5.2g, Protein: 34.2g

SNACKS & DESSERTS

Grilled Fruit Skewers

Servings: 6

Ingredients:

- 8 strawberries, large
- 2 peaches, sliced thick
- 1 pear, sliced thick
- 1 cup pineapple, cubed
- 1 banana, sliced thick

Directions:

1. Preparing the Ingredients.
2. Skewer the cut fruit.
3. Grilling
4. Grill to desired doneness. Dipping sauce: in a saucepot, bring the heavy cream to a boil. Add the chocolate chips and remove from heat. Mix until creamy, then add vanilla. Serve grilled fruit with chocolate dipping sauce. Chocolate Dipping Sauce 1 cup heavy cream, 1 cup semi-sweet chocolate chips ½ tsp. vanilla extract. Feel free to choose any chocolate you like. Dark and white work well with this recipe.

Banana "tostones" With Cinnamon Rum Whipped Cream

Servings: 4

Cooking Time: 3 Minutes

Ingredients:

- FOR THE WHIPPED CREAM:
- 1 cup heavy (whipping) cream
- 3 tablespoons confectioners' sugar
- 1 tablespoon dark rum
- 1 teaspoon ground cinnamon
- FOR THE BANANAS:
- ⅔ cup granulated sugar
- 1 tablespoon ground cinnamon
- 2 teaspoons very finely grated lemon or lime zest
- 4 bananas, chilled in the refrigerator for 1 hour
- 4 tablespoons (½ stick) unsalted butter, melted
- Cooking oil spray
- Fresh mint sprigs (optional), for garnish

Directions:

1. Preparing the Ingredients

2. Make the whipped cream: Place the cream in a chilled mixer bowl or in a large metal bowl. Beat with a mixer until soft peaks form, starting on the slow speed and gradually increasing the speed to high. The total beating time will 6 to 8 Minutes. When soft peaks have formed, add the confectioners' sugar, rum, and cinnamon. Continue beating the cream until stiff peaks form, about 2 Minutes longer. Don't overbeat the cream or it will start to turn to butter. The cinnamon rum whipped cream can be made several hours ahead. Refrigerate it, covered, until ready to serve.

3. Prepare the bananas: Place the granulated sugar, cinnamon, and lemon zest in a shallow bowl and stir to mix.

4. When ready to cook, bring the griddle grill to medium-low heat Lightly coat the grill surface with cooking oil spray. Arrange the pieces of banana upright on the grill, pressing down to flatten the bananas. Grill the bananas until they are crusty and golden brown, 3 to 5 Minutes. After 2 Minutes, brush the tops of the bananas with any remaining butter, and sprinkle any remaining cinnamon sugar over them.

5. Meanwhile, peel the bananas and cut each crosswise into 1-inch pieces. Dip the ends of each piece of banana in the melted butter, then in the cinnamon sugar, shaking off the excess.

6. Place the banana "tostones" on plates. Garnish each serving with a large dollop of cinnamon rum whipped cream and a mint sprig, if using, and serve at once.

Tasty Herb Mushrooms

Servings: 4

Cooking Time: 10 Minutes

Ingredients:

- 1 lb mushroom caps
- 1 tbsp basil, minced
- 1 garlic clove, minced
- 1/2 tbsp vinegar
- 1/2 tsp ground coriander
- 1 tsp rosemary, chopped
- Pepper

- Salt

Directions:

1. Preheat the griddle to high heat.
2. Spray griddle top with cooking spray.
3. Add all ingredients into the bowl and toss well.
4. Add mushroom mixture onto the hot griddle top and cook until mushroom is tender.
5. Serve and enjoy.

Nutrition Info: (Per Serving): Calories 25 ;Fat 0.4 g ;Carbohydrates 4 g ;Sugar 2 g ;Protein 3.6 g ;Cholesterol 0 mg

Grilled Apple Bowls

Servings: 4

Ingredients:

- Simple Syrup
- 1 cup sugar
- 1 cup water
- 1 cinnamon stick
- 2 apples, large

Directions:

1. Preparing the Ingredients.
2. Simple syrup: in a saucepan, bring the sugar, water, and cinnamon stick to a boil. Set aside.
3. Cut the apples in half and core with a melon baller. Add to the hot simple syrup. Arrange apples on the Grill Pan, cut side down.
4. Grilling
5. Cook for 3 Minutes. Turn over and continue grilling until tender. Baste with simple syrup. Top the apples with ice cream, caramel sauce, and chopped pecans immediately before serving. 2 cups vanilla ice cream ½ cup caramel sauce ½ cup pecans, chopped. These apples can also be made in advance. After grilling, cool in the refrigerator. When you are ready to serve, warm up in the microwave.

Straw Berries Pizza

Servings: 8

Ingredients:

- 1 (8-oz.) thin crust pizza dough ¼ cup caramel sauce
- 2 bananas, sliced & grilled
- 8 strawberries, halved & grilled

- 2 tbsp. chocolate sauce

Directions:

1. Preparing the Ingredients.
2. Arrange pizza dough to fit onto the Grill Pan. Cook on both sides to desired doneness.
3. Grilling
4. Spread caramel sauce over the pizza. Layer with bananas and strawberries. Spry with chocolate and raspberry sauces. Top with peanuts. Cut pizza into 8 slices. Serve alone or with your favorite ice cream. 2 tbsp. raspberry sauce ¼ cup peanuts, chopped. Sprinkling toasted coconut or crumbled graham crackers will add extra flavor and crunch!

Ranch Potatoes

Servings: 2

Cooking Time: 12 Minutes

Ingredients:

- 1/2 lb baby potatoes, wash and cut in half
- 1/4 tsp garlic powder
- 1/2 tbsp olive oil
- 1/4 tsp dill
- 1/4 tsp chives
- 1/4 tsp parsley
- 1/4 tsp paprika
- 1/4 tsp onion powder
- Salt

Directions:

1. Preheat the griddle to high heat.
2. Spray griddle top with cooking spray.
3. Add all ingredients into the mixing bowl and toss well.
4. Spread potatoes on hot griddle top and cook until tender.
5. Serve and enjoy.

Nutrition Info: (Per Serving): Calories 100 ;Fat 3.7 g ;Carbohydrates 14.8 g ;Sugar 0.2 g ;Protein 3.1 g ;Cholesterol 0 mg

Grilled Cinnamon S'mores Toast

Servings: 4

Cooking Time: 2 Minutes

Ingredients:

- 1/2 cup sugar

- 1 tbsp. cinnamon
- 4 slices bread 1/4 cup margarine
- 15 baby marshmallows
- 1 (4.4-oz.) chocolate bar

Directions:

1. Combine sugar and cinnamon in a bowl.
2. Spread margarine over one side of each slice of bread. Sprinkle with cinnamon and sugar mixture.
3. Arrange two slices of bread onto the Griddle Grill Pan, margarine side down. Cover each slice with marshmallows and half of the chocolate bar.
4. Top with remaining two slices of bread. Use Grill Press to cook on both sides, 3 minutes per side.
5. Serve alone or with a tall glass of milk!

Nutrition Info: (Per serving):354.3 calories; 20g fat; 5.7 g protein; 54.1 g carbs

Yummy Turkey Burger

Servings: 6
Cooking Time: 14 Minutes
Ingredients:
- 1 lb ground turkey
- 1 egg, lightly beaten
- 1 cup Monterey jack cheese, grated
- 1 cup carrot, grated
- 1 cup cauliflower, grated
- 2 garlic cloves, minced
- 1/2 cup onion, minced
- 3/4 cup breadcrumbs
- Pepper
- Salt

Directions:

1. Preheat the griddle to high heat.
2. Spray griddle top with cooking spray.
3. Add all ingredients into the mixing bowl and mix until well combined.
4. Make small patties from mixture and place on hot griddle top and cook until golden brown from both sides.
5. Serve and enjoy.

Nutrition Info: (Per Serving): Calories 299 ;Fat 15.5 g ;Carbohydrates 13.8 g ;Sugar 2.7 g ;Protein 2.7 g ;Cholesterol 121 mg

Jelly Pancake

Servings: 4
Ingredients:
- Pancakes
- 2 eggs
- 1 ½ cups whole milk ½ cup smooth peanut butter
- 1 ¼ cups pancake mix
- Peanut Butter Cream ½ cup smooth peanut butter
- 1 (8-oz.) container whipped topping
- Grape Syrup ¼ cup grape jelly

Directions:

1. Preparing the Ingredients.
2. Griddle Recipe
3. Grilling
4. Preheat the Griddle Pan over medium heat. Make pancake batter: Beat together the egg and milk. Add the peanut butter and Beat until smooth. Mix in the pancake mix. Peanut butter cream: Beat together the peanut butter and whipped topping. Grape syrup: combine the jelly and syrup. Microwave until melted, about 20 seconds. Mix to combine. Ladle a half cup of the pancake batter onto the Pan. Cook until golden brown, about 2 Minutes per side. Continue until all batter is used up. Stack the pancakes, spreading a smear of the peanut butter cream between each pancake. Spry with the grape syrup before serving. ½ cup maple syrup.

Figs With Walnuts And Honey

Servings: 4
Cooking Time: 10 Minutes
Ingredients:
- 8 ripe figs, stemmed
- 2 tablespoons walnut oil or good-quality olive oil
- 8 walnut halves, toasted
- ¼ cup honey

Directions:

1. Preparing the Ingredients
2. Brush the figs with the walnut oil, then cut an X in the stem ends. Push 1 walnut half into each fig.
3. Bring the griddle grill to medium-low heat. Oil the griddle and allow it to heat until the oil is

shimmering but not smoking. Put the figs on the grill grate, stem side up, and cook until the fruit softens, 5 to 10 Minutes. Transfer to a platter, drizzle with the honey, and serve.

Grilled Nectarines With Blackberries And Mascarpone

Servings: 2
Cooking Time: 3 Minutes
Ingredients:
- 2 tablespoons honey
- 2 large ripe nectarines, quartered
- ½ teaspoon ground cinnamon
- 1pint blackberries, blueberries, raspberries, or strawberries (if using strawberries, thinly slice them)
- ¼ cup mascarpone

Directions:
1. Preparing the Ingredients
2. Spoon the honey into a small shallow baking dish. Dip the nectarine sections into the honey and then sprinkle the flesh side with the cinnamon.
3. Bring the griddle grill to medium-low heat. Oil the griddle and allow it to heat until the oil is shimmering but not smoking. Grill the nectarines, flesh side down, for about 3 Minutes, until the flesh is crisp, hot, and browned. Serve the nectarines in shallow bowls, topped with the berries and a spoonful of mascarpone.
Nutrition Info: (Per Serving): CALORIES: 162; FAT:7G; PROTEIN:1G

Pineapple–star Fruit Skewers With Orange-clove Syrup

Servings: 4
Cooking Time: 16 Minutes
Ingredients:
- ½ cup sugar
- Zest of 1 large orange, taken off in strips
- 1 tablespoon whole cloves
- 1 small pineapple
- 3 star fruit

Directions:
1. Preparing the Ingredients
2. Put the sugar, orange zest, cloves, and ½ cup water in a small saucepan over medium heat; stir until the sugar dissolves. Bring to a boil, reduce the heat, and gently bubble for 5 to 10 Minutes. Remove from the heat and let sit for at least 30 Minutes and up to several hours to let the flavor develop. When you are happy with the flavor of the syrup, strain it and use or refrigerate in an airtight container; it will keep for at least a week.
3. If you're using bamboo or wooden skewers, soak them in water for 30 Minutes.
4. Trim, peel, and core the pineapple, then cut it into 2-inch chunks. Cut the star fruit into ½-inch-thick slices. Skewer the fruit; using 2 skewers makes them easier to turn. Skewer the star fruit through the points of the star on two sides. Brush lightly with the orange-clove syrup.
5. Bring the griddle grill to medium-high heat. Oil the griddle and allow it to heat until the oil is shimmering but not smoking. Put the skewers on the grill, and cook, until the pineapple chunks brown in spots, 6 to 8 Minutes per side; brush the fruit several times with the syrup while it grills. When the fruit is done, brush it once more with syrup. Transfer to a platter and serve hot or warm.

Grilled Doughnut With Ice Cream

Servings: 4
Ingredients:
- 4 apple cider doughnuts, sliced in half
- 2 pears, halved, cored & sliced
- 4 cups vanilla ice cream ½ cup chocolate sauce whipped cream, for serving

Directions:
1. Preparing the Ingredients.
2. Arrange doughnut and pears halves on the Grill Pan.
3. Grilling
4. Cook to desired doneness. Place the ice cream in a small baking pan and cover with plastic wrap. Press flat, about 2 inches thick, then place the pan into the freezer. Cut frozen ice cream into 8 discs the same size as the doughnuts. Place one doughnut half on each dish. Layer with sliced pears and ice cream. Top with a second doughnut half. Repeat to make it a triple decker. Spry with chocolate sauce and whipped

cream before serving. The key to this recipe is to use the best seasonal fruit. Local orchards and farm stands will keep the variety of this recipe endless!

Rum-soaked Pineapple

Servings: 6
Cooking Time: 15 Minutes
Ingredients:
- 1/2 cup packed brown sugar
- 1/2 cup rum
- 1 teaspoon ground cinnamon
- 1 pineapple, cored and sliced
- cooking spray
- vanilla ice cream

Directions:
1. Mix the rum with brown sugar and cinnamon in a mixing bowl.
2. Pour this mixture over your pineapple rings and mix well.
3. Let the pineapple rings soak for about 15 minutes and flip the rings after 7 minutes.
4. Prepare and preheat your Griddle Grill setting it at a High-temperature setting.
5. Once your grill is preheated, place your pineapple rings on the grill.
6. Grill it for 4 minutes per side.
7. Serve your pineapple rings with a scoop of ice cream on top.
Nutrition Info: (Per serving): Calories: 143.2 Fat: 0.4g Carbs: 21g Protein: 0.3g

Banana Coconut Fritters

Servings: 16
Ingredients:
- 2 bananas, mashed
- 1/3 cup flour ½ tsp. cinnamon
- 2 eggs ½ cup shredded coconut

Directions:
1. Preparing the Ingredients.
2. Combine all ingredients except oil in a bowl. Preheat Griddle Pan for 4 Minutes on medium heat. Coat the Pan with canola oil. Drop heaping tablespoons of fritter batter onto the Pan.
3. Grilling

4. Cook until golden on each side before serving. ½ tsp. baking powder 1 tbsp. brown sugar, 1 tbsp. milk, 3 tbsp. canola oil.

Grilled Banana Sundae

Servings: 2
Ingredients:
- Strawberry Sauce
- 8 oz. strawberries
- 2 tsp. sugar
- Pineapple Sauce 8 oz. pineapple rounds ¼ cup light brown sugar
- Sundae Basics

Directions:
1. Preparing the Ingredients.
2. Strawberry sauce: in a small saucepan, combine the grilled strawberries with sugar.
3. Grilling
4. Grill strawberries, pineapple, and banana halves to desired doneness. Set aside. Cook until sugar is dissolved and strawberries are blended. Pineapple sauce: in a separate saucepan, combine the grilled pineapples with light brown sugar. Cook until sugar is dissolved and pineapples are blended. Assemble the sundae: line a dish with grilled bananas. Top with 3 scoops vanilla and / or chocolate ice cream and fruit sauces. Sprinkle with peanuts. Top with chocolate sauce and whipped cream before serving. bananas, halved lengthwise vanilla ice cream chocolate ice cream chocolate sauce ½ cup peanuts, chopped whipped cream. I love using this grilled fruit sauce to flavor my margaritas!

Sugared Peaches With Candied Ginger Ice Cream

Servings: 4
Cooking Time: 20 Minutes
Ingredients:
- 1 pint vanilla ice cream, softened just a bit
- ¼ cup chopped candied ginger
- 2 or 4 ripe peaches, depending on their size
- 4 tablespoons (½ stick) butter, melted
- ¼ cup Demerara sugar, or more as needed
- Fresh mint sprigs for garnish

Directions:
1.   Preparing the Ingredients
2.   Put the ice cream and ginger in a bowl and mash together with a wooden spoon until the ginger is mixed throughout the ice cream. This can be done several days ahead; put it back in the ice cream container and freeze at least a couple hours.
3.   When you're ready for dessert, cut the peaches in half through the stem end and remove the pits. Brush with the melted butter. Put the sugar on a plate and dredge the cut side of each peach in it.
4.   Bring the griddle grill to medium-low heat. Oil the griddle and allow it to heat until the oil is shimmering but not smoking. Put the peaches on the grill, cut side up, and cook until they soften, 10 to 15 Minutes. Turn them cut side down and cook until the sugar caramelizes to a golden brown, 2 to 5 Minutes. Transfer to a platter. To serve, put the warm peaches on plates or in dessert bowls, cut side up. Divide the ice cream between them, or pass the ice cream at the table. Garnish with the mint.

Parmesan Zucchini Patties

Servings: 6
Cooking Time: 30 Minutes
Ingredients:
- 1 cup zucchini, shredded and squeeze out all liquid
- 1/2 tbsp Dijon mustard
- 1 egg, lightly beaten
- 1/4 tsp red pepper flakes
- 1/4 cup parmesan cheese, grated
- 1/2 tbsp mayonnaise
- 1/2 cup breadcrumbs
- 2 tbsp onion, minced
- Pepper
- Salt

Directions:
1.   Add all ingredients into the bowl and mix until well combined.
2.   Preheat the griddle to high heat.
3.   Spray griddle top with cooking spray.
4.   Make small patties from the zucchini mixture and place on hot griddle top and cook until golden brown from both sides.

5.   Serve and enjoy.
Nutrition Info: (Per Serving): Calories 156 ;Fat 7.7 g ;Carbohydrates 7.9 g ;Sugar 1.2 g ;Protein 10.5 g ;Cholesterol 48 mg

Grilled Pineapple Rings With Ice Cream

Servings: 4
Cooking Time: 4 Minutes
Ingredients:
- 1 whole pineapple, sliced into 6 equal slices
- 6 scoops vanilla bean ice cream
- 6 spoonfuls of whipped cream
- ¼ cup almond slivers, toasted
- ¼ cup sweetened shredded coconut, toasted
- ½ cup caramel sauce
- mint (to garnish)

Directions:
1.   Preparing the Ingredients
2.   Bring the griddle grill to medium-low heat. Oil the griddle and allow it to heat until the oil is shimmering but not smoking. Grill pineapple until a nice char forms, about 2 Minutes per side.
3.   Remove pineapple from grill, top each slice with a scoop of ice cream, a dollop of whipped cream, almonds, and coconut.
4.   Drizzle each with caramel sauce, garnish with mint, and serve.

Cauliflower Zucchini Fritters

Servings: 4
Cooking Time: 8 Minutes
Ingredients:
- 2 medium zucchini, grated and squeezed
- 1 tbsp olive oil
- 1/4 cup coconut flour
- 3 cups cauliflower rice
- 1/2 tsp sea salt

Directions:
1.   Add all ingredients except oil into the bowl and mix until well combined.
2.   Preheat the griddle to high heat.
3.   Add oil to the hot griddle top.

4. Make small patties from the mixture and place onto the griddle top and cook for 3-4 minutes on each side.

5. Serve and enjoy.

Nutrition Info: (Per Serving): Calories 90 ;Fat 5 g ;Carbohydrates 8.8 g ;Sugar 5 g ;Protein 4.3 g ;Cholesterol 0 mg

Grilled Pear Crisp

Servings: 4

Ingredients:

- 2 pears, cored
- Crisp Topping ¼ cup brown
- sugar ¼ cup flour
- 3 tbsp. butter

Directions:

1. Preparing the Ingredients.

2. Grill pears until tender. About 5 Minutes per side. Make crisp topping: combine brown sugar, flour, butter, walnuts, and cinnamon in a bowl.

3. Grilling

4. Bake in the oven for 15 Minutes at 400° F. Place half a pear into each serving bowl. Immediately before serving, top with ½ cup vanilla ice cream, 2 tbsp. crisp topping, and 1 tbsp. caramel sauce. 2 tbsp. walnuts ½ tsp. cinnamon, 2 cups vanilla ice cream 4 tbsp. caramel sauce. Feel free to substitute any fruit that is ripe and in season such as local apples or peaches.

Sweet Potato Pancakes

Servings: 2

Ingredients:

- Wet ¾ cup sweet potato, cooked & pureed
- 2 eggs
- 1 cup buttermilk
- 3 tbsp. butter, melted, for batter

Directions:

1. Preparing the Ingredients.

2. Mix the wet ingredients together and set aside. In a bowl, mix all dry ingredients together. Combine wet Ingredients and dry ingredients. Preheat Griddle Pan on medium heat and melt 2 tbsp. butter.

3. Grilling

4. Cook pancakes to desired doneness. Serve with walnut or pecan syrup and bananas. Dry

5. 1 cup flour, 2 tsp. baking powder ½ tsp. salt ½ tsp. cinnamon ¼ tsp. nutmeg, 1 tbsp. brown sugar, 2 tbsp. butter, for Grilling. To Serve walnut or pecan syrup bananas. Griddle Recipe

Grilled Cinnamon Toast

Servings: 2

Ingredients:

- ½ cup sugar
- 1 tbsp. cinnamon
- 4 slices bread ¼ cup margarine
- 15 baby marshmallows
- 1 (4.4-oz.) chocolate bar

Directions:

1. Preparing the Ingredients.

2. Combine sugar and cinnamon in a bowl. Spread margarine over one side of each slice of bread. Sprinkle with cinnamon and sugar mixture. Arrange two slices of bread onto the Grill Pan, margarine side down. Cover each slice with marshmallows and half of the chocolate bar. Top with remaining two slices of bread.

3. Grilling

4. Use Grill Press to cook on both sides, 3 Minutes per side. Serve alone or with a tall glass of milk! As if this couldn't get any better, try a little peanut butter inside!

Grilled Berry Cobbler

Servings: 2

Cooking Time: 20 Minutes

Ingredients:

- 2 cans (21-ounces) pie filling, raspberry flavor
- vanilla ice cream
- 1 (8-ounces) package of cake mix
- 1/2 cup olive oil
- 1-1/4 cups water

Directions:

1. Mix your cake mix with olive oil and water in a bowl until smooth.

2. Place a foil packet on the working surface along with pie filling.

3. Spread your cake mix on top of the pie filling.
4. Cover your foil packet and seal it.
5. Preheat your indoor grill on the medium temperature setting.
6. Once your grill is preheated, place the foil package on the grill.
7. Close the grill lid and set to "Bake Mode" for 20 minutes.
8. Serve with vanilla ice cream and enjoy!
Nutrition Info: (Per serving): Calories: 319 Fat: 11.9g Carbs: 14.8g Protein: 5g

Pineapple Sundae

Servings: 2
Ingredients:
- ¼ pineapple
- peeled & sliced 2 cups vanilla ice cream
- ¼ cup whipped cream

Directions:
1. Preparing the Ingredients.
2. Let cool before chopping.
3. Grilling
4. Grill the pineapple until tender. Scoop ice cream into 2 serving dishes. Immediately before serving, top with pineapple, whipped cream, and sliced almonds. ¼ cup sliced almonds. You can also make an awesome dessert "salsa" by adding chopped strawberries and fresh mint.

Whoopie Pies

Servings: 8
Ingredients:
- 1 /3 cup cocoa powder
- 1 ½ cup flour
- 1 tsp. baking soda ½ tsp. salt ¾ cup buttermilk ¾ cup butter ¾ cup brown sugar
- 1 egg ½ tsp. vanilla extract
- Marshmallow Cream Filling

Directions:
1. Preparing the Ingredients.
2. Griddle Recipe
3. Grilling
4. Preheat the oven to 350° F. In a bowl, sift the cocoa powder, flour, baking soda, and salt.

5. In an electric mixer, cream the buttermilk, butter, and brown sugar together. Add the egg and vanilla. Mix until incorporated. Slowly add the flour mixture to the creamed ingredients. Blend. Make first batch of cake halves: arrange eight ¼ cup scoops of cake mix onto the Griddle Pan. Bake 12-15 Minutes or until done. Repeat step 6 to make second batch of cake halves. In the mixer, cream the butter and confectioners' sugar together until creamy. Add the marshmallow and vanilla. Place the marshmallow cream in a piping bag and fill the whoopie pies. ¾ stick butter,1 cup confectioners' sugar, 1 2/3 cup marshmallow cream, 1 tsp. vanilla extract.

Flavors Cauliflower Bites

Servings: 4
Cooking Time: 10 Minutes
Ingredients:
- 1 lb cauliflower florets
- 1 tsp ground coriander
- 1/2 tsp dried rosemary
- 1 1/2 tsp garlic powder
- 1 tbsp olive oil
- 1 tsp sesame seeds
- Pepper
- Salt

Directions:
1. Preheat the griddle to high heat.
2. Spray griddle top with cooking spray.
3. Add cauliflower florets and remaining ingredients into the bowl and toss well and spread on the hot griddle top.
4. Cook cauliflower florets until tender.
5. Serve and enjoy.
Nutrition Info: (Per Serving): Calories 65 ;Fat 4 g ;Carbohydrates 7.1 g ;Sugar 3 g ;Protein 2.6 g ;Cholesterol 0 mg

Marshmallow Stuffed Banana

Servings: 1
Cooking Time: 5 Minutes
Ingredients:
- 1 banana
- 1/4 cup chocolate chips

- 1/4 cup mini marshmallows

Directions:

1. Take the peeled banana and spread over a 12×12-inch foil sheet.
2. Slice a slit in the banana lengthwise and stuff the slit with chocolate chips and marshmallows.
3. Wrap some foil around the banana to seal it.
4. Prepare and preheat your Griddle Grill set to the medium temperature setting.
5. Once the grill is preheated and place the banana in the grill.
6. Grill each side for 5 minutes.
7. Unwrap your yummy treat, serve and enjoy it!

Nutrition Info: (Per serving): Calories: 372 Fat: 11.8g Carbs: 45.8g Protein: 4g

Piña Colada Tacos

Servings: 4

Cooking Time: 10 Minutes

Ingredients:

- ½ ripe pineapple, peeled, cored, and cut into 1-inch cubes
- ¼ cup dark rum
- ¼ cup coconut milk
- 4 tablespoons (½ stick) butter, softened
- 4 7-inch flour tortillas
- 1 tablespoon sugar, or as needed
- Lime wedges for serving (optional)
- ½ cup shredded coconut, toasted

Directions:

1. Preparing the Ingredients
2. 1 Put the pineapple, rum, and coconut milk in a bowl and toss to combine. Let the fruit macerate for at least 20 Minutes, or up to several hours in the refrigerator.
3. If you're using bamboo or wooden skewers, soak them in water for 30 Minutes.
4. Spread the butter on both sides of the tortillas, then sprinkle with the sugar. Thread the pineapple cubes onto 4 skewers, letting excess marinade drip back in the bowl.
5. 2 Bring the griddle grill to medium-high heat. Oil the griddle and allow it to heat until the oil is shimmering but not smoking. Put the skewers on the grill and cook until the pineapple is caramelized, 5 to

8 Minutes per side. Transfer the skewers to a platter. Put the tortillas on the grill, and cook, turning once, until they lightly brown, 1 to 2 Minutes per side.

6. To serve, put a skewer on top of each tortilla, squeeze with some lime if you like, and sprinkle with toasted coconut. To eat, pull out the skewer.

Strawberries Romanoff

Servings: 4

Cooking Time: 5 Minutes

Ingredients:

- 1 pound strawberries, hulled
- ¼ cup sugar
- 2 tablespoons Grand Marnier
- 1 pint vanilla ice cream

Directions:

1. Preparing the Ingredients
2. Gently toss the strawberries with the sugar to coat.
3. Bring the griddle grill to medium-low heat. Oil the griddle and allow it to heat until the oil is shimmering but not smoking. Put them on the griddle and cook, rolling them around once, until heated through, about 5 Minutes total.
4. Transfer the strawberries to a bowl. Cut them in halves or quarters, depending on their size, and toss with the Grand Marnier. Let them macerate while you spoon out the ice cream, then divide between the bowls and serve, pouring any liquid from the bowl over the top.

Strawberry Shortcake

Servings: 6

Ingredients:

- 1 angel food cake, sliced into wedges
- ½ stick butter 1 lb. strawberries, cut in half zest of 1 lemon juice of ½ lemon
- Strawberry Shortcake

Directions:

1. Preparing the Ingredients.
2. Brush the cake wedges with butter.
3. Grilling
4. Grill to desired doneness. Grill the strawberries. Let cool before tossing with lemon zest, lemon juice,

and 1 tbsp. sugar. Whip the cream with ¼ cup confectioners' sugar and vanilla. Top cake wedges with strawberries and whipped cream immediately before serving. 1 tbsp. sugar 1 ½ cup heavy cream, ¼ cup confectioners' sugar, to whip cream 1 tsp. vanilla extract. I've diced the grilled angel food cake and turned this into an amazing layered trifle when making dessert for a large group!

Watermelon With Honey And Lime

Servings: 4
Cooking Time: 8 Minutes
Ingredients:
- 2 1- to 1½-inch-thick watermelon slices, halved
- Salt
- ¼ cup honey
- Lime wedges for serving

Directions:
1. Preparing the Ingredients
2. Lightly salt the watermelon on both sides, then brush both sides with the honey.
3. Bring the griddle grill to medium-low heat. Oil the griddle and allow it to heat until the oil is shimmering but not smoking. Put the slices on the griddle and cook, turning once, until the watermelon browns in spots, 4 Minutes per side. Transfer to a cutting board. Cut the slices into quarters or smaller wedges. Serve with the lime wedges.

Grilled Peanut Butter Banana Split

Servings: 4
Cooking Time: 10 Minutes
Ingredients:
- 4 ripe bananas
- 1 cup peanut butter baking chips
- 1 cup mini marshmallows
- ¼ cup brown sugar

Directions:
1. Preparing the Ingredients
2. Leaving banana in peel, slice down the length of the banana, but don't cut it in half.
3. Pry apart the bananas and evenly distribute brown sugar inside each banana.
4. On top of the brown sugar, evenly distribute the peanut butter chips.
5. On top of peanut butter chips, place the mini marshmallows.
6. Bring the griddle grill to medium-low heat. Oil the griddle and allow it to heat until the oil is shimmering but not smoking. Place bananas in grill, and cook for 10 Minutes or until peanut better chips have melted and marshmallows are toasted.
7. Remove and serve hot.

Grilled Peaches With Honey

Servings: 4
Cooking Time: 5 Minutes
Ingredients:
- fresh peaches
- fresh honey
- cinnamon to taste
- coconut oil
- plain yogurt or ice cream for topping

Directions:
1. Preparing the Ingredients
2. Slice the peaches lengthwise top to bottom and remove the pits.
3. Drizzle honey on the cut side of the peach and sprinkle with cinnamon.
4. Bring the griddle grill to medium-low heat. Oil the griddle and allow it to heat until the oil is shimmering but not smoking. Set the peaches sliced-side up and grill peaches for a couple Minutes cut side down then flip and brush with coconut oil honey and cinnamon
5. Grill for several Minutes until the skin is starting to brown and pull back.
6. Serve with vanilla ice cream while still warm.

Buttermilk Angel Biscuits

Servings: 14 Biscuits
Cooking Time: 15 Minutes
Ingredients:
- 2½ cups all-purpose flour, plus more for kneading
- 2¼ teaspoons (1 package) instant yeast
- 1 teaspoon baking powder

- 1 teaspoon baking soda
- 1 teaspoon salt
- 8 tablespoons (1 stick) butter, melted, plus softened butter for the pans
- 1 cup buttermilk

Directions:

1. Preparing the Ingredients
2. 1 Whisk the flour, yeast, baking powder and soda, and salt together in a large bowl. Stir the melted butter into the buttermilk, then add to the flour and stir it in. With your hands, gather the dough into a ball and transfer to a lightly floured work surface. Knead the dough until smooth, 1 to 2 Minutes, then pat it down to a ½- to ¾-inch thickness. Cut the biscuits using a 2½-inch cutter. Pat the scraps together, flatten again, and cut more biscuits.
3. Coat the insides of two 12-inch cast-iron skillets with softened butter. Put the biscuits in the pans, not touching. Cover with plastic wrap and let rise until doubled, 1 to 1½ hours.
4. 2 Bring the griddle grill to medium-low heat. Oil the griddle and allow it to heat until the oil is shimmering but not smoking. Put the pans on the grill, and bake until the bottoms of the biscuits release easily and are golden brown and the tops have browned in spots, 5 to 7 Minutes per side. The biscuits should be springy to the touch, and a toothpick inserted in the center should come out clean. Transfer the biscuits to a clean dish towel or napkin, wrap loosely, and serve warm.

Caramelized Five-spice Oranges

Servings: 4
Cooking Time: 8 Minutes
Ingredients:

- ¼ cup sugar
- ½ teaspoon five-spice powder
- 2 large oranges
- ¼ cup chopped fresh mint

Directions:

1. Preparing the Ingredients
2. Stir the sugar and five-spice powder together on a small plate. Cut a sliver off the top and bottom of each orange so that it will sit flat on the grates without rolling, then turn them on their sides and cut

in half through the equator. Remove any seeds. Press the cut side of each half into the sugar. Let sit until the sugar is absorbed and/or you are ready to grill.
3. Bring the griddle grill to medium-low heat. Oil the griddle and allow it to heat until the oil is shimmering but not smoking. Put the orange halves on the grill, sugared side up, and cook until they are warm all the way through, 6 to 8 Minutes, Turn them over and cook just until the cut sides brown, 2 to 3 Minutes. Transfer to individual serving plates, sprinkle with the mint, and serve with a knife and fork or with grapefruit spoons, if you have them.

Grilled Peaches Cinnamon

Servings: 4
Cooking Time: 5 Minutes
Ingredients:

- 4 ripe peaches, halved and pitted
- 1/4 cup salted butter
- 1 teaspoon granulated sugar
- 1/4 teaspoon cinnamon

Directions:

1. Mix your sugar, butter and cinnamon in a bowl until smooth.
2. Preheat your griddle grill on the medium temperature setting.
3. Once your grill is preheated, place the peaches on the grill.
4. Grill it for 1 minute per side.
5. Serve the peaches with cinnamon butter on top and enjoy!

Nutrition Info: (Per serving): Calories: 46.4 Fat: 0.1g Carbs: 54.7g Protein: 0.7g

Stuffed French Toast

Servings: 2
Cooking Time: 6 Minutes
Ingredients:

- 2 loaves of French bread, cut into 1-inch slices
- For the custard
- ¼ cup milk
- 1 egg
- juice of ½ blood orange
- 3 strawberries, stemmed and hulled

- pinch of ground cloves
- ¼ tsp. vanilla
- pinch of sea salt
- For the filling
- ¼ cup mascarpone
- zest of 1 blood orange
- 1 tsp. real maple syrup
- sliced strawberries
- powdered sugar

Directions:

1. Preparing the Ingredients
2. Mix the custard ingredients together in a blender, and set aside in a bowl.
3. Mix the mascarpone, blood orange zest, and maple syrup together in a bowl.
4. Add the mascarpone mixture and the sliced strawberries between two slices of French bread. Dip the outsides of the sandwich in the custard and drip the remaining custard off.
5. Bring the griddle grill to medium-low heat. Oil the griddle and allow it to heat until the oil is shimmering but not smoking. Cook for 5–6 Minutes until the custard is lightly golden brown and the bread is golden.
6. Dust with powdered sugar and enjoy.

Grill-baked Apple

Servings: 1
Cooking Time: 10 Minutes
Ingredients:

- 1 apple
- 1 tablespoon butter, softened
- 1 tablespoon brown sugar
- ⅛ teaspoon ground cinnamon, or more to taste

Directions:

1. Preparing the Ingredients
2. Remove the core of the apple carefully, without puncturing the bottom or side. Mash the butter, brown sugar, and cinnamon with the back of a fork until thoroughly mixed. Stuff the mixture into the cavity of the apple.
3. Bring the griddle grill to medium-low heat. Oil the griddle and allow it to heat until the oil is shimmering but not smoking. Put the apple on the griddle, and cook until it feels soft when gently squeezed and the filling is melted, 8 to 10 Minutes, depending on its size. Transfer to plate and let cool a few Minutes before serving.

VEGETABLE & SIDE DISHES

Tomato Melts With Spinach Salad

Servings: 4
Cooking Time: 6 Minutes
Ingredients:
- 1 or 2 large fresh tomatoes (enough for 4 thick slices across)
- 2 tablespoons good-quality olive oil, plus more for brushing
- Salt and pepper
- 2 teaspoons white wine vinegar
- 1 teaspoon Dijon mustard
- 3 cups baby spinach
- 6 slices cheddar cheese (about 4 ounces)

Directions:
1. Preparing the Ingredients
2. Core the tomatoes and cut 4 thick slices (about 1 inch); save the trimmings. Brush them with oil and sprinkle with salt and pepper on both sides. Whisk the 2 tablespoons oil, vinegar, and mustard together in a bowl. Chop the trimmings from the tomatoes; add them to the dressing along with the spinach and toss until evenly coated.
3. Bring the griddle grill to medium-high heat. Oil the griddle and allow it to heat until the oil is shimmering but not smoking. Put the tomato slices and cook for 3 Minutes. Turn the tomatoes and top each slice with a slice of cheddar, and cook until the cheese is melted, 2 to 3 Minutes. Transfer to plates and serve with the salad on top.

Asian-spiced Grilled Squash

Servings: 4
Cooking Time: 6 Minutes
Ingredients:
- 1½ pounds butternut or other winter squash
- 2 tablespoons (¼ stick) unsalted butter
- 2 cloves garlic, minced
- 1 scallion, both white and green parts, minced
- 1 tablespoon black or white sesame seeds
- 2 tablespoons maple syrup
- 1 tablespoon soy sauce

Directions:
1. Preparing the Ingredients
2. Peel the squash and remove and discard the seeds. Cut the squash crosswise into ½-inch-thick slices. Place the butter in a small saucepan and melt it over medium heat. Add the garlic, scallion, and sesame seeds and cook until the garlic has lost its rawness, about 1 minute; do not let the garlic brown. Stir in the maple syrup and soy sauce, bring to a boil, and let boil for 30 seconds.
3. When ready to cook, brush the squash slices on both sides with some of the butter mixture.
4. Bring the griddle grill to medium-high heat. Oil the griddle and allow it to heat until the oil is shimmering but not smoking. Place the squash on the hot grill. The squash will be done after cooking 4 to 6 Minutes. You will need to turn the squash so that you can baste both side until browned and tender; it should be easy to pierce with a knife. Baste the squash once or twice with the garlic mixture as it cooks.
5. Transfer the squash to a platter or plates and serve at once, spooning any remaining butter mixture and, if cooked in a contact grill, any juices that collected in the drip pan over it.

Zucchini Antipasto

Servings: 4
Cooking Time: 6 Minutes
Ingredients:
- ¼ cup olive oil
- 3 garlic cloves, minced
- 1 tablespoon fresh thyme leaves or ½ teaspoon dried thyme
- ¼ teaspoon salt
- ¼ teaspoon freshly ground black pepper
- 4 medium zucchini, cut lengthwise into ¼-inch-thick slices
- 1 tablespoon balsamic vinegar

Directions:
1. Preparing the Ingredients
2. Whisk together the olive oil, garlic, thyme, salt, and pepper in a large bowl.
3. Add the zucchini and toss to coat.

4. Bring the griddle grill to medium-high heat. Oil the griddle and allow it to heat until the oil is shimmering but not smoking.

5. Grill for about 6 Minutes, until the zucchini slices have taken on grill marks and are very tender.

6. Serve either hot off the grill or at room temperature, sprinkled with the vinegar.

Nutrition Info: (Per Serving): CALORIES: 156; FAT:14G; PROTEIN:2G

Radishes With Butter And Sea Salt

Servings: 6

Cooking Time: 6 Minutes

Ingredients:

- 1 pound whole radishes, with greens attached
- 2 tablespoons good-quality olive oil
- 8 tablespoons (1 stick) butter, softened
- 1 to 2 tablespoons sea salt

Directions:

1. Preparing the Ingredients

2. Trim the root ends and remove any discolored leaves from the radishes. Rinse, pat them dry with paper towels, and toss with the oil until completely coated, including the greens.

3. Bring the griddle grill to medium-high heat. Oil the griddle and allow it to heat until the oil is shimmering but not smoking. Put the radishes on the grill, and cook until they warm through and char in places, 4 to 6 Minutes. Transfer to a platter and serve with the butter and salt in small bowls for dipping.

Stir Fry Bok Choy

Servings: 4

Cooking Time: 5 Minutes

Ingredients:

- 2 heads bok choy, trimmed and cut crosswise
- 1 tsp sesame oil
- 2 tsp soy sauce
- 2 tbsp water
- 1 tbsp butter
- 1 tbsp peanut oil
- 1 tbsp oyster sauce
- 1/2 tsp salt

Directions:

1. In a small bowl, mix together soy sauce, oyster sauce, sesame oil, and water and set aside.

2. Preheat the griddle to high heat.

3. Add oil to the hot griddle top.

4. Add bok choy and salt and stir fry for 2 minutes.

5. Add butter and soy sauce mixture and stir fry for 1-2 minutes.

6. Serve and enjoy.

Nutrition Info: (Per Serving): Calories 122 ;Fat 8.2 g ;Carbohydrates 9.5 g ;Sugar 5 g ;Cholesterol 8 mg

Eggplant Salad With Yogurt And Tomatoes

Servings: 4

Cooking Time: 10 Minutes

Ingredients:

- 1 large eggplant (1½ pounds)
- ¼ cup good-quality olive oil, plus more for brushing
- Salt and pepper
- 1½ cups yogurt
- 1 or 2 cloves garlic, minced, to taste
- ¼ cup chopped scallions
- ¼ cup chopped fresh mint
- 1 tablespoon fresh lemon juice, or to taste
- 1 large or 2 medium fresh tomatoes, cut into bite-sized chunks
- Ground sumac for garnish (optional)

Directions:

1. Preparing the Ingredients

2. Peel the eggplant if you like; cut it into ¾-inch slices. Brush with the oil and sprinkle with salt and pepper to taste on both sides.

3. Bring the griddle grill to medium-high heat. Oil the griddle and allow it to heat until the oil is shimmering but not smoking. Put the eggplant on the grill and cook until the slices develop deep grill marks and are tender, 10Minutes; brush the eggplant with more oil if it starts to look dry. Transfer to a cutting board and chop into bite-sized pieces.

4. Put the yogurt, garlic, scallions, mint, and lemon juice in a large bowl and stir to combine. (You can prepare the recipe to this point up to a day before; cover and refrigerate the eggplant and yogurt mixture separately.)

5. Add the tomatoes and eggplant to the yogurt and stir to coat. Serve chilled or bring to room temperature and garnish with sumac if you like.

Grilled Corn With Soy Butter And Sesame

Servings: 4
Cooking Time: 18 Minutes
Ingredients:
- 3 tablespoons unsalted butter
- 1 scallion, both white and green parts, finely chopped
- 2 tablespoons soy sauce
- 4 ears sweet corn, shucked and cut or broken in half crosswise
- 1 tablespoon toasted sesame seeds

Directions:
1. Preparing the Ingredients
2. Melt the butter in a saucepan over medium heat. Add the scallion and cook until it loses its rawness, about 1 minute (you don't want the scallion to brown). Stir in the soy sauce and remove the saucepan from the heat.
3. Bring the griddle grill to medium-high heat. Oil the griddle and allow it to heat until the oil is shimmering but not smoking.
4. Arrange the ears of corn on the hot Grill. The corn will be done after cooking 2 to 3 Minutes per side (8 to 12 Minutes in all) until nicely browned on all sides, basting it with a little of the soy butter. Use a light touch as you baste; you don't want to drip a lot of butter into the grill.
5. Transfer the corn to a platter. Brush it with any remaining soy butter, sprinkle the sesame seeds over it, and serve at once.
6. To toast sesame seeds, place them in a dry cast-iron or other heavy skillet (don't use a nonstick skillet for this). Cook the sesame seeds over medium heat until lightly browned, about 3 Minutes, shaking the skillet to ensure that they toast evenly. Transfer the toasted sesame seeds to a heatproof bowl to cool.

Grilled Summer Squash

Servings: 12
Cooking Time: 10 Minutes

Ingredients:
- 1 Summer Squash
- 2 tbsps. Olive Oil
- Sea Salt To Taste

Directions:
1. Slice the squash in half lengthwise. Brush the squash with the olive oil and season with salt.
2. Heat the griddle grill to medium heat, and set the squash cut-side down. Cook for 5 minutes per side until it is tender.
3. Remove from heat and serve.
Nutrition Info: (Per serving):Calories 74, Fat 5.4g, protein 10g, carbs 6.1g

Stir Fry Vegetables

Servings: 4
Cooking Time: 20 Minutes
Ingredients:
- 2 medium potatoes, cut into small pieces
- 3 medium carrots, peeled and cut into small pieces
- 1/4 cup olive oil
- 1 small rutabaga, peeled and cut into small pieces
- 2 medium parsnips, peeled and cut into small pieces
- Pepper
- Salt

Directions:
1. Preheat the griddle to high heat.
2. In a large bowl, toss vegetables with olive oil.
3. Transfer vegetables onto the hot griddle top and stir fry until vegetables are tender.
4. Serve and enjoy.
Nutrition Info: (Per Serving): Calories 218 ;Fat 12.8 g ;Carbohydrates 25.2 g ;Sugar 6.2 g ;Protein 2.8 g ;Cholesterol 0 mg

Stuffed Cabbage With Summer Vegetables

Servings: 4
Cooking Time: 12 Minutes
Ingredients:
- 2 tablespoons good-quality olive oil, plus more for brushing and drizzling

- 1 onion, chopped
- Salt and pepper
- 2 tablespoons minced garlic
- 1 cup thinly sliced snow peas
- 1 cup chopped summer squash
- 1 cup fresh or frozen corn kernels
- 1 large head green or Savoy cabbage (about 4 pounds)
- ¼ cup chopped fresh basil
- Grated zest of 1 lime

Directions:

1. Preparing the Ingredients
2. 1 Put the oil in a large skillet over medium-high heat. When it's hot, add the onion, sprinkle with salt and pepper, and cook, stirring occasionally, until it's soft, about 5 Minutes. Add the garlic and stir until fragrant, about another minute. Add the snow peas, squash, and corn and cook, stirring occasionally, until the squash is just tender, about 5 Minutes. Season to taste with salt and pepper. Remove from the heat.
3. 2 Use a thin-bladed sharp knife to cut a cone-shaped wedge out of the bottom of the cabbage, removing its core. Pull off 12 large, untorn, unblemished leaves and put in a steamer above a couple inches of salted water (you may need to work in batches). Cover and cook until the leaves are just flexible enough to bend, about 5 Minutes. Drain and rinse under cold water to stop the cooking. (Reserve the remaining cabbage leaves for another use.)
4. 3 Stir the basil and lime zest into the filling; taste and adjust the seasoning. To stuff the cabbage leaves, put the leaves, concave side up, on a work surface or cutting board. Make a V-cut in each leaf to remove the tough central stem. Put a heaping ¼ cup or so of filling in the center of a leaf, just above where you cut out the stem. Fold over the sides, then roll up from the stem end, making a little package (like a burrito). Don't roll too tightly; you'll quickly get the hang of it. Skewer the rolls with a toothpick or 2 to hold them together or just put them on a platter seam side down. (You can make the stuffed cabbage to this point up to a day or 2 in advance; cover and refrigerate.)
5. 4 Bring the griddle grill to medium-high heat. Oil the griddle and allow it to heat until the oil is shimmering but not smoking. Brush the rolls with oil on all sides and sprinkle with salt. Put the rolls and

cook 6 Minutes, to heat the filling. Transfer to a platter, drizzle with a little more oil, and serve.

Easy Fried Rice

Servings: 2
Cooking Time: 10 Minutes
Ingredients:

- 4 cups rice, cooked
- 2 large eggs
- 2 tbsp green onion, sliced
- 2 tbsp olive oil
- 1 tsp salt

Directions:

1. In a bowl, whisk eggs and set aside.
2. Preheat the griddle to high heat.
3. Spray griddle top with cooking spray.
4. Add cooked rice on hot griddle top and fry until rice separate from each other.
5. Push rice to one side of the griddle top. Add oil to the griddle and pour beaten egg.
6. Add salt and mix egg quickly with rice and cook until rice grains are covered by egg.
7. Add green onion and stir fry for 2 minutes.
8. Serve and enjoy.

Nutrition Info: (Per Serving): Calories 557 ;Fat 19.8 g ;Carbohydrates 79.6 g ;Sugar 0.7 g ;Protein 14 g ;Cholesterol 186 mg

Grilled Yellow Potatoes

Servings: 4
Cooking Time: 50 Minutes
Ingredients:

- Yellow Potatoes
- Olive Oil
- Sea Salt And Black Pepper To Taste
- Paprika

Directions:

1. Slice the potatoes in half lengthwise, and place them into a large bag or bowl.
2. Drizzle them with olive oil, and stir or shake to coat the potatoes.
3. Add the salt, pepper, and paprika to taste, and stir or shake until completely combined.

4.	Preheat the griddle grill to medium, and spray it with oil.

5.	Place the potatoes sliced-side down, and grill for several minutes or until you can see grill marks and they feel tender on the cut side.

6.	Turn the potatoes over and grill until they are tender through.

7.	Remove from heat and serve.

Nutrition Info: (Per serving):Calories 280, Fat 11g, carbs 8g, Protein 4g

Pineapple Fried Rice

Servings: 4

Cooking Time: 10 Minutes

Ingredients:

- 3 cups cooked brown rice
- 1/2 cup frozen corn
- 2 carrots, peeled and grated
- 1 onion, diced
- 2 garlic cloves, minced
- 2 tbsp olive oil
- 1/2 tsp ginger powder
- 1 tbsp sesame oil
- 3 tbsp soy sauce
- 1/4 cup green onion, sliced
- 1/2 cup ham, diced
- 2 cups pineapple, diced
- 1/2 cup frozen peas

Directions:

1.	In a small bowl, whisk soy sauce, ginger powder, and sesame oil and set aside.

2.	Preheat the griddle to high heat.

3.	Add oil to the hot griddle top.

4.	Add onion and garlic and sauté for 3-4 minutes.

5.	Add corn, carrots, and peas and stir constantly for 3-4 minutes.

6.	Stir in cooked rice, green onions, ham, pineapple, and soy sauce mixture and stir continuously for 2-3 minutes.

7.	Serve and enjoy.

Nutrition Info: (Per Serving): Calories 375 ;Fat 13.3 g ;Carbohydrates 57.6 g ;Sugar 12.7 g ;Protein 9.4 g ;Cholesterol 10 mg

Stuffed Winter Squash With Quinoa, Green Beans, And Tomatoes

Servings: 4

Cooking Time: 45 Minutes

Ingredients:

- ¾ cup quinoa
- 2 or 4 winter squash
- 2 tablespoons good-quality olive oil, plus more for brushing and drizzling
- Salt and pepper
- 1 cup chopped cherry or grape tomatoes
- ½ cup thinly sliced green beans (cut across into rounds)
- 2 tablespoons chopped fresh parsley
- 5 cloves garlic, minced

Directions:

1.	Preparing the Ingredients

2.	Put the quinoa in a saucepan with 1½ cups water, bring to a boil, reduce the heat so the water bubbles gently but steadily, cover, and cook undisturbed until the surface is dotted with holes and the water is almost all absorbed, about 15 Minutes. Turn off the heat and let stand until the kernels are tender and fluffy, 5 to 10 Minutes.

3.	Cut the squash in half. If necessary, take a thin slice off the uncut side so the squash half sits on the work surface without rocking. Remove the seeds with a spoon, serrated grapefruit spoon, or melon baller. Brush the interior and cut surface with oil; for varieties with edible skin, also brush the skin. Sprinkle all over with salt and pepper.

4.	Bring the griddle grill to medium-high heat. Oil the griddle and allow it to heat until the oil is shimmering but not smoking. Put the squash on the griddle skin side down, and cook until the flesh is just fork tender, 25 Minutes. Turn them cut side down to brown, about 5 Minutes. Transfer to a plate, cut side up.

5.	While the squash are on the grill, finish the filling. Put the quinoa, tomatoes, green beans, parsley, garlic, and 2 tablespoons oil in a bowl; sprinkle with salt and pepper and toss with a fork until combined. Cover to keep warm. (You can prepare the filling and partially cook the squash earlier in the day; cover and refrigerate until you're ready to grill; cooking time may be a bit longer.)

6. If necessary, heat the grill for medium direct cooking. Divide the filling between the squash halves. Return to the grill and cook until the filling is hot, 10 to 15 Minutes. Transfer to a platter, drizzle the tops with a little oil if you like, and serve.

Grilled Artichokes With Honey Dijon

Servings: 4-6
Cooking Time: 30 Minutes
Ingredients:
- 6 whole artichokes
- 1/2 gallon water
- 3 Tbsp. sea salt
- olive oil
- sea salt to taste
- 1/4 cup raw honey
- 1/4 cup boiling water
- 3 Tbsp. Dijon mustard

Directions:
1. Cut the artichokes in half lengthwise top to bottom.
2. Mix the 3 tablespoons of sea salt and water together. Place the artichokes in the brine for 30 minutes to several hours before cooking.
3. Heat the griddle grill to medium.
4. Remove the artichokes from the brine, drizzle with olive oil on the cut side, and season with sea salt.
5. Grill for 15 minutes on each side, cut side down first.
6. Turn the grill down to low, and turn the artichokes cut-side down while you mix the honey, boiling water, and Dijon.
7. Turn the artichokes back over, and brush the Dijon mix well over the cut side until it is all absorbed.
8. Serve alongside a protein like salmon, beef, pork, or chicken, or with rice or potatoes for a vegetarian option.
Nutrition Info: (Per serving):Calories 601kcal, Fat 57g, Protein 8g, Carbs 21g

Italian Zucchini Slices

Servings: 4
Cooking Time: 5 Minutes

Ingredients:
- 2 zucchini, cut into 1/2-inch thick slices
- 1 tsp Italian seasoning
- 2 garlic cloves, minced
- 1/4 cup butter, melted
- 1 1/2 tbsp fresh parsley, chopped
- 1 tbsp fresh lemon juice
- Pepper
- Salt

Directions:
1. In a small bowl, mix melted butter, lemon juice, Italian seasoning, garlic, pepper, and salt.
2. Brush zucchini slices with melted butter mixture.
3. Preheat the griddle to high heat.
4. Place zucchini slices on the griddle top and cook for 2 minutes per side.
5. Transfer zucchini slices on serving plate and garnish with parsley.
6. Serve and enjoy.
Nutrition Info: (Per Serving): Calories 125 ;Fat 12 g ;Carbohydrates 4.1 g ;Sugar 1.9 g ;Protein 1.5 g ;Cholesterol 31 mg

Portobello Caprese Stacks

Servings: 4
Cooking Time: 12 Minutes
Ingredients:
- 4 portobello mushrooms, stems removed and caps wiped clean
- 6 tablespoons good-quality olive oil
- Salt and pepper
- 24 large fresh basil leaves
- 4 tomato slices (each about ¾ inch thick; 2 large tomatoes)
- 4 slices fresh mozzarella cheese (about 4 ounces)
- Balsamic Syrup for serving

Directions:
1. Preparing the Ingredients
2. Brush the mushrooms with the oil and sprinkle with salt and pepper on both sides.
3. Bring the griddle grill to medium-high heat. Oil the griddle and allow it to heat until the oil is shimmering but not smoking. Put the mushrooms and cook until well browned and tender, 6 to 8 Minutes.

4.   Transfer the mushrooms to a platter, gill side up. Cover the top with the basil, then add the tomato slices, and finally the mozzarella. Return the stacks directly over the grill, close the lid, and cook until the cheese melts, 2 to 4 Minutes. Serve hot or at room temperature, drizzled with balsamic syrup.

Grilled Eggplant With Feta And Lemon

Servings: 4
Cooking Time: 15 Minutes
Ingredients:
- 1 large eggplant, cut into ½-inch slices
- 1 tablespoon salt
- 3 tablespoons olive oil
- 4 ounces feta cheese, crumbled
- ½ teaspoon sweet paprika
- Freshly ground black pepper
- 1 lemon, cut in half

Directions:
1.   Preparing the Ingredients
2.   Spread the eggplant slices on a rimmed baking sheet and sprinkle with half of the salt. Flip the slices and sprinkle with the remaining salt. Let sit for 15 Minutes to take away some of the bitterness of the eggplant. Transfer the slices to sheets of paper towels and pat dry.
3.   Bring the griddle grill to medium-high heat. Oil the griddle and allow it to heat until the oil is shimmering but not smoking. Brush both sides of the eggplant slices with the olive oil. Grill for about 6 Minutes, until the slices have taken on grill marks and are golden brown.
4.   Transfer the eggplant to a serving platter and top with the feta, paprika, some pepper, and a squirt of lemon juice. Serve hot or at room temperature.
Nutrition Info: (Per Serving): CALORIES: 204; FAT:17G; PROTEIN:6G

Chiles Rellenos With Charred Green Enchilada Sauce

Servings: 4
Cooking Time: 35 Minutes
Ingredients:
- 1¼ pounds tomatillos, husked and rinsed
- 5 large poblano or other mild fresh green chiles
- 3 tablespoons good-quality olive oil
- 2 large onions, chopped
- 5 cloves garlic, minced
- 1 teaspoon dried oregano
- 1 cup vegetable broth or water
- Salt and pepper
- 3 cups grated or shredded Chihuahua or Monterey Jack cheese
- ½ cup chopped fresh cilantro
- ¼ cup fresh lime juice
- Crumbled queso fresco for garnish

Directions:
1.   Preparing the Ingredients
2.   1 Bring the griddle grill to medium-high heat. Oil the griddle and allow it to heat until the oil is shimmering but not smoking. Put the tomatillos and 1 of the poblanos on the griddle, and cook the tomatillos until the skins are lightly browned and blistered, 10 to 15 Minutes. Cook the poblano until it's blackened, 15 to 20 Minutes. When the vegetables are done, transfer them a bowl) When the poblano is cool enough to handle, remove the skin, stem, and seeds. Chop by hand along with the tomatillos, saving the juices.
3.   2 Put the oil in a large, deep skillet over medium heat, add the onions and garlic, and cook, stirring occasionally, until quite soft and golden, 10 to 15 Minutes. Add the tomatillos and poblano, oregano, broth, and a large pinch of salt and pepper; stir and bring to a gentle bubble. Cook, stirring occasionally, until the mixture is slightly thickened, 10 to 15 Minutes. Remove from the heat. Use an immersion blender to purée the sauce in the pan, or very carefully transfer it to a blender, purée, and return it to the pan.
4.   Cut a slit into one side of each of the remaining poblanos, from the stem down to the tip. Carefully remove the seeds without ripping the chiles, then stuff them with the Chihuahua or Jack cheese.
5.   3 Heat the grill for medium. Put the chiles on the griddle, slit side facing up so the cheese doesn't melt out, and cook until the skins have blistered and the flesh is tender, 10 to 15 Minutes. Transfer to a platter. Stir the cilantro and lime juice into the sauce; taste and adjust the seasonings. Spoon the sauce over the chiles, sprinkle with queso fresco, and serve.

Eggplant Parmesan With Grill-roasted Tomato Sauce

Servings: 4
Cooking Time: 24 Minutes
Ingredients:
- I bet.
- 2 eggplants (¾ to 1 pound each)
- 5 tablespoons good-quality olive oil
- 2 tablespoons balsamic vinegar
- Salt and pepper
- 6 cups cherry or grape tomatoes
- 1 cup freshly grated Parmesan cheese
- About 1 cup packed fresh basil leaves
- 7 ounces mozzarella cheese, thinly sliced

Directions:
1. Preparing the Ingredients
2. Peel the eggplant if you like, and cut each lengthwise into 4 slices not more than ¾ inch thick each. Whisk 4 tablespoons of the oil and the vinegar together with some salt and pepper in a small bowl. Brush the eggplant slices with the oil mixture on both sides. Put them on a baking sheet until you're ready to grill them.
3. Toss the tomatoes with the remaining 1 tablespoon oil and either skewer them or put them in a perforated grill pan and spread them into a single layer.
4. Bring the griddle grill to medium-high heat. Oil the griddle and allow it to heat until the oil is shimmering but not smoking. Put the tomatoes on the grill and cook, turning the skewers or shaking the pan several times, until they start to look wrinkled and get a bit charred in places, 7 to 8 Minutes total. Don't let them cook too long; they should be saucy when you cut them up. Transfer the tomatoes to a bowl.
5. Put the eggplant on the grill and cook until the slices are browned and tender, 10 Minutes.
6. While the eggplant is cooking, chop the tomatoes by hand on a cutting board or in the bowl with an immersion blender, leaving the sauce somewhat chunky. If you chopped by hand, transfer the tomatoes and any juices back to the bowl. Sprinkle the sauce with salt and pepper; taste and adjust the seasoning.
7. As the eggplant is ready, transfer the slices to a platter. Top each slice with 2 tablespoons Parmesan, a layer of basil leaves, and a layer of mozzarella. Return the slices to grill, close the lid, and cook until the mozzarella melts, 4 to 5 Minutes. Return the eggplant to the platter. Reheat the tomato sauce if you like, top the eggplant with the sauce, and serve.

Fire-roasted Tomatillo Salsa With Grilled Tortilla Wedges

Servings: 2 Cups
Cooking Time: 10 Minutes
Ingredients:
- 1 pound tomatillos
- 3 scallions, trimmed
- 1 jalapeño chile, seeded and minced
- 2 cloves garlic, minced, or to taste
- ¼ cup chopped fresh cilantro
- 3 tablespoons fresh lime juice, or to taste
- Salt and pepper
- 8 small corn or flour tortillas
- Good-quality olive oil for brushing

Directions:
1. Preparing the Ingredients
2. Remove the husks from the tomatillos, then rinse off the tacky residue and pat dry.
3. Bring the griddle grill to high heat. Oil the griddle. Put the tomatillos and scallions on the grill, and cook until they soften and blacken in spots, turning them to cook evenly, 5 to 10 Minutes total. Transfer to a food processor or blender and add the jalapeño, garlic, cilantro, lime juice, and some salt and pepper; pulse a few times until the mixture comes together but isn't completely smooth. Taste and adjust the seasoning, adding more garlic or lime if you like.
4. Brush the tortillas on both sides with oil. Put them on the grill directly over the fire, close the lid, and toast, turning once, until they are warm and grill marks develop, 1 to 2 Minutes per side. Cut into wedges and serve with the salsa.

Baba Ghanoush

Servings: 6
Cooking Time: 30 Minutes
Ingredients:
- 2 medium-large eggplants (about 2 pounds total), with stems on
- ⅓ cup tahini
- ¼ cup fresh lemon juice
- 2 large cloves garlic, or to taste, minced
- Salt and pepper
- 4 pita breads for serving
- Good-quality olive oil for drizzling
- ¼ cup chopped fresh parsley for garnish

Directions:
1. Preparing the Ingredients
2. Pierce the eggplants in several places with a thin knife or skewer.
3. Bring the griddle grill to high heat. Oil the griddle. Put them on the grill. Cook until the eggplants are blackened on all sides and collapsed, 25 to 30 Minutes. Transfer to a bowl.
4. Whisk the tahini and lemon juice in a small bowl until smooth. Stir in the garlic and sprinkle with salt and pepper.
5. When the eggplants are cool enough to handle, peel off and discard the burnt skin. Mash the flesh with a fork. Beat in the tahini mixture until the dip is smooth. Taste and adjust the seasoning. (You can make the dip up to 3 days in advance; cover and refrigerate.)
6. Toast the pita directly over the grill, turning once, until they're warm and have grill marks, 1 to 2 Minutes per side. Cut into wedges. Transfer the baba ghanoush to a shallow serving bowl, drizzle the top with olive oil, sprinkle with the parsley, and serve with the warm pita wedges.

Roasted Tomatoes With Hot Pepper Sauce

Servings: 4-6
Cooking Time: 120 Minutes
Ingredients:
- 2 lbs. tomatoes; Roma fresh
- 1 lb. spaghetti
- 2 tbsps. chopped garlic
- 1/2 cup olive oil
- 3 tbsps. chopped parsley
- Salt, hot pepper and black pepper, to taste

Directions:
1. Set the griddle grill to preheat and push the temperature to 400 degrees F.
2. Now take the tomatoes, wash them thoroughly and cut them into halves; lengthwise.
3. Place it on a baking dish while making sure that the cut side faces upwards
4. Sprinkle it with chopped parsley, salt, black pepper, and garlic.
5. Also, put 1/4 cup of olive oil over them
6. Now place it on the grill for 1-1/2 hour
7. The tomatoes will shrink, and the skin is likely to get slightly blackened
8. Now remove the tomatoes from the baking dish and place it on the food processor and puree it well
9. Drop the pasta into the boiling salt water and cook it until it turns tender
10. Drain and toss it immediately with the pureed tomatoes mix
11. Now add the leftover 1/4 cup of raw olive oil along with crumbled hot pepper as per taste
12. Toss well and serve

Nutrition Info: (Per serving):Calories 45, Fat 1g, Carbs 8g, Protein 2g

Grilled Eggplant Napoleon

Servings: 4
Cooking Time: 5 Minutes
Ingredients:
- 1 Eggplant sliced lengthwise into half inch slices
- Olive Oil brushed
- Salt to taste
- Heirloom Tomatoes sliced thin
- Lemon squeezed
- Balsamic Vinegar drizzled
- Fresh Basil garnished
- Haloumi cheese sliced to 1/4 inch thick and grilled

Directions:
1. Slice the eggplant thin lengthwise and brush with the olive oil and season with the sea salt.
2. Slice the Halloumi to 1/4 inch and grill on high for one minute per side

3.   Turn the griddle grill on high and grill the eggplant for several minutes per side until the grill marks are prevalent.

4.   Layer with the eggplant with grilled halloumi, and sliced tomatoes. Squeeze the lemon juice over the top, drizzle the balsamic vinegar, and garnish with slightly torn fresh basil.

Nutrition Info: (Per serving):Calories 232.4, Fat 6.7 g, carbs 9g, Protein 11.2 g

Watermelon Steaks With Rosemary

Servings: 4
Cooking Time: 10 Minutes
Ingredients:

- 1 small watermelon
- ¼ cup good-quality olive oil
- 1 tablespoon minced fresh rosemary
- Salt and pepper
- Lemon wedges for serving

Directions:

1.   Preparing the Ingredients

2.   Cut the watermelon into 2-inch-thick slices, with the rind intact, and then into halves or quarters, if you like. If there are seeds, use a fork to remove as many as you can without tearing up the flesh too much.

3.   Put the oil and rosemary in a small bowl, sprinkle with salt and pepper, and stir. Brush or rub the mixture all over the watermelon slices. (You can prepare the watermelon for the grill up to 2 hours ahead; wrap tightly in plastic wrap to keep it from drying out and refrigerate.)

4.   Bring the griddle grill to medium-high heat. Oil the griddle and allow it to heat until the oil is shimmering but not smoking. Put the watermelon on the griddle and cook, turning once, until the flesh develops grill marks and has dried out a bit, 4 to 5 Minutes per side. Transfer to a platter and serve with lemon wedges.

Grilled Brussels Sprouts With Balsamic Glaze

Servings: 4
Cooking Time: 10 Minutes

Ingredients:

- brussels sprouts
- olive oil
- sea salt to taste
- balsamic vinegar

Directions:

1.   Preparing the Ingredients

2.   Cut the sprouts in half lengthwise from top to bottom.

3.   Brush with olive oil and season with sea salt.

4.   Bring the griddle grill to medium-high heat. Oil the griddle and allow it to heat until the oil is shimmering but not smoking. Grill the sprouts cut-side down for 5 Minutes on each side. Brush the sprouts lightly with balsamic, and grill for a minute or so more to set the vinegar before serving.

Simplest Grilled Asparagus

Servings: 4
Cooking Time: 10 Minutes
Ingredients:

- 1½–2 pounds asparagus
- 1–2 tablespoons good-quality olive oil or melted butter
- Salt

Directions:

1.   Preparing the Ingredients

2.   Cut the tough bottoms from the asparagus. If they're thick, trim the ends with a vegetable peeler. Toss with the oil and sprinkle with salt.

3.   Bring the griddle grill to medium-high heat. Oil the griddle and allow it to heat until the oil is shimmering but not smoking. Put the asparagus on the griddle and cook until the thick part of the stalks can barely be pierced with a skewer or thin knife, 8 to 10 Minutes total. Transfer to a platter and serve.

Sautéed Vegetables

Servings: 4
Cooking Time: 5 Minutes
Ingredients:

- 2 medium zucchini, cut into matchsticks
- 2 tbsp coconut oil
- 2 tsp garlic, minced

- 1 tbsp honey
- 3 tbsp soy sauce
- 1 tsp sesame seeds
- 2 cups carrots, cut into matchsticks
- 2 cups snow peas

Directions:

1. In a small bowl, mix together soy sauce, garlic, and honey and set aside.
2. Preheat the griddle to high heat.
3. Add oil to the hot griddle top.
4. Add carrots, snow peas, and zucchini, and sauté for 1-2 minutes.
5. Add soy sauce mixture and stir fry for 1 minute.
6. Garnish with sesame seeds and serve.

Nutrition Info: (Per Serving): Calories 160 ;Fat 7.5 g ;Carbohydrates 20.2 g ;Sugar 12.1 g ;Protein 5.3 g ;Cholesterol 0 mg

Cauliflower With Garlic And Anchovies

Servings: 4
Cooking Time: 10 Minutes
Ingredients:

- 1 head cauliflower (1½–2 pounds)
- 6 tablespoons good-quality olive oil
- 6 oil-packed anchovy fillets, chopped, or more to taste
- 1 tablespoon minced garlic
- ½ teaspoon red chile flakes, or to taste
- (optional)
- Salt and pepper (optional)
- Chopped fresh parsley for garnish

Directions:

1. Preparing the Ingredients
2. 1 Break or cut the cauliflower into florets about 1½ inches across; put in a bowl.
3. Put the oil, anchovies, garlic, and red pepper if using it in a small skillet over medium-low heat. Cook, stirring occasionally, until the anchovies begin to break up and the garlic just begins to color, about 5 Minutes. Taste and add more anchovies or some salt and pepper. Pour half of the oil mixture over the cauliflower; toss to coat evenly with it. Bring the griddle grill to medium-high heat. Oil the griddle and allow it to heat until the oil is shimmering but not smoking. Put the florets in a single and cook until the cauliflower is as tender and browned as you like it, 5 Minutes for crisp-tender to 10 Minutes for fully tender. Transfer to a serving bowl, drizzle over the remaining sauce and the parsley, toss gently, and serve warm or at room temperature.

Bacon-wrapped Maple-cinnamon Carrots

Servings: 4
Cooking Time: 30 Minutes
Ingredients:

- ½ cup maple syrup
- 1 Tbsp. fresh ground cinnamon
- 2 lb. carrots (uniform in size, washed and peeled)
- 1 lb. thin-cut bacon
- pinch of salt
- 1 Tbsp. finely chopped parsley, for garnish

Directions:

1. Preparing the Ingredients
2. Whisk together the syrup and cinnamon.
3. Lightly coat carrots with cinnamon-syrup mixture; a basting brush works well for this task.
4. Spiral wrap each carrot with one slice of bacon. Depending on the size of the carrot, two slices may be needed.
5. Apply another coat of the cinnamon-syrup to the outside of the bacon and sprinkle with a pinch of salt.
6. Bring the griddle grill to high heat. Oil the griddle. Place carrots. Ensure you lay the carrots with the tips of the bacon tucked under the carrots to prevent them from unraveling.
7. Reapply another coat of the cinnamon-syrup, and cook additional 15 Minutes or until bacon is crisp and carrots are firm but cooked.
8. Remove from grill, drizzle with any remaining cinnamon-syrup, garnish with parsley, and serve.

Prosciutto-wrapped Melon

Servings: 8
Cooking Time: 6 Minutes
Ingredients:

- 1 ripe cantaloupe
- Salt and pepper
- 16 thin slices prosciutto

Directions:

1.   Preparing the Ingredients
2.   1 Cut the cantaloupe in half lengthwise and scoop out all the seeds. Cut each half into 8 wedges, then cut away the rind from each wedge. Sprinkle with salt and pepper and wrap each wedge with a slice of prosciutto, covering as much of the cantaloupe as possible.
3.   2 Bring the griddle grill to medium-high heat. Oil the griddle and allow it to heat until the oil is shimmering but not smoking. Put the wedges and cook until the prosciutto shrivels, browns, and crisps in places, 4 to 6 Minutes. Serve hot or at room temperature.

Easy Seared Green Beans

Servings: 6
Cooking Time: 10 Minutes
Ingredients:
- 1 1/2 lbs green beans, trimmed
- 1 1/2 tbsp rice vinegar
- 3 tbsp soy sauce
- 1 1/2 tbsp sesame oil
- 2 tbsp sesame seeds, toasted
- 1 1/2 tbsp brown sugar
- 1/4 tsp black pepper

Directions:
1.   Cook green beans in boiling water for 3 minutes and drain well.
2.   Transfer green beans to chilled ice water and drain again. Pat dry green beans.
3.   Preheat the griddle to high heat.
4.   Add oil to the hot griddle top.
5.   Add green beans and stir fry for 2 minutes.
6.   Add soy sauce, brown sugar, vinegar, and pepper and stir fry for 2 minutes more.
7.   Add sesame seeds and toss well to coat.
8.   Serve and enjoy.
Nutrition Info: (Per Serving): Calories 100 ;Fat 5 g ;Carbohydrates 11.7 g ;Sugar 3.9 g ;Protein 3.1 g ;Cholesterol 0 mg

Grilled Zucchini Squash Spears

Servings: 6
Cooking Time: 15 Minutes

Ingredients:
- 4 midsized zucchini
- 2 springs thyme with the leaves pulled out
- 1 tbsp. sherry vinegar
- 2 tbsps. olive oil
- Salt and pepper as per your taste

Directions:
1.   Take the zucchini and cut off the ends
2.   Now cut each of them in a half and then cut every half into thirds
3.   Take all the leftover ingredients in a midsized zip lock bag and then add spears to it
4.   Toss it and mix well so that it coats the zucchini
5.   Start the griddle grill to preheat to medium high
6.   Remove the spears from the bag and place them directly on the grill grate. Make sure that the side faces downwards
7.   Cook for 3 to 4 minutes per side until you can see the grill starts popping up and the zucchini should become tender too
8.   Remove from the grill and add more thyme leaves if needed
9.   Serve and enjoy
Nutrition Info: (Per serving):Calories 235, Carbs 21g, Fat 16g, Protein 8g

Crisp Baby Artichokes With Lemon Aïoli

Servings: 4
Cooking Time: 10 Minutes
Ingredients:
- 2 tablespoons good-quality olive oil
- Grated zest and juice of 1 lemon
- 8 baby artichokes
- ½ cup mayonnaise
- 1 teaspoon minced garlic, or more to taste
- Salt and pepper

Directions:
1.   Preparing the Ingredients
2.   1 Whisk the oil and lemon juice in a large bowl. Peel away and discard the outer layers of each artichoke until the leaves are half yellow and half green. With a sharp knife, cut across the top of the artichoke to remove the green tops. Leave 1 inch of stem and use a paring knife or vegetable peeler to trim the bottom so no green remains. Cut the

artichoke in half lengthwise from top to bottom. As each artichoke is trimmed, add it to the olive oil mixture and toss to coat evenly; this helps delay discoloring. (You can cover the bowl and refrigerate for up to several hours.)

3.   2 Make the aïoli: Put the mayonnaise, garlic, and lemon zest in a small bowl, sprinkle with salt and pepper, and whisk to combine. Taste and adjust the seasoning.

4.   3 Bring the griddle grill to medium-high heat. Oil the griddle and allow it to heat until the oil is shimmering but not smoking. Put the artichokes cut side down on the grill and cook until tender and charred, 8 to 10 Minutes. Transfer to a plate and serve with the aïoli for dipping.

Grilled Tempeh

Servings: 4
Cooking Time: 6 Minutes
Ingredients:
- 1 8-ounce piece tempeh
- Good-quality olive oil for brushing
- Salt
- Pepper (optional)

Directions:
1.   Preparing the Ingredients
2.   Brush the tempeh with oil and sprinkle with salt on both sides.
3.   Bring the griddle grill to high heat. Oil the griddle Put the tempeh and cook until it develops a crust and releases easily from the grates, about 6. Sprinkle with more salt and some pepper if you like, and serve.

Healthy Zucchini Noodles

Servings: 4
Cooking Time: 10 Minutes
Ingredients:
- 4 small zucchini, spiralized
- 1 tbsp soy sauce
- 2 onions, spiralized
- 2 tbsp olive oil
- 1 tbsp sesame seeds
- 2 tbsp teriyaki sauce

Directions:
1.   Preheat the griddle to high heat.
2.   Add oil to the hot griddle top.
3.   Add onion and sauté for 4-5 minutes.
4.   Add zucchini noodles and cook for 2 minutes.
5.   Add sesame seeds, teriyaki sauce, and soy sauce and cook for 4-5 minutes.
6.   Serve and enjoy.
Nutrition Info: (Per Serving): Calories 124 ;Fat 8.4 g ;Carbohydrates 11.3 g ;Sugar 5.7 g ;Protein 3.2 g ;Cholesterol 0 mg

Stir Fry Cabbage

Servings: 4
Cooking Time: 5 Minutes
Ingredients:
- 1 cabbage head, tear cabbage leaves, washed and drained
- 2 green onion, sliced
- 1 tbsp ginger, minced
- 2 garlic cloves, minced
- 1 tbsp soy sauce
- 1/2 tbsp vinegar
- 4 dried chilies
- 2 tbsp olive oil
- 1/2 tsp salt

Directions:
1.   Preheat the griddle to high heat.
2.   Add oil to the hot griddle top.
3.   Add ginger, garlic, and green onion and sauté for 2-3 minutes.
4.   Add dried chilies and sauté for 30 seconds.
5.   Add cabbage, vinegar, soy sauce, and salt and stir fry for 1-2 minutes over high heat until cabbage wilted.
6.   Serve and enjoy.
Nutrition Info: (Per Serving): Calories 115 ;Fat 7.3 g ;Carbohydrates 12.7 g ;Sugar 6 g ;Protein 2.9 g ;Cholesterol 0 mg

Roasted Asparagus

Servings: 4
Cooking Time: 7 Minutes
Ingredients:

- 1 pound medium to thin asparagus, woody stems snapped off and discarded
- 2 tablespoons olive oil
- ¼ teaspoon salt
- ½ teaspoon freshly ground black pepper
- ¼ cup grated Parmesan cheese, preferably freshly grated

Directions:

1. Preparing the Ingredients
2. Toss the asparagus with the olive oil, salt, and pepper in a medium bowl.
3. Bring the griddle grill to medium-high heat. Oil the griddle and allow it to heat until the oil is shimmering but not smoking. Grill the asparagus spears for about 7 Minutes, until they have taken on grill marks and are tender.
4. Serve hot or at room temperature, sprinkled with the Parmesan.

Nutrition Info: (Per Serving): CALORIES: 102; FAT:9G; PROTEIN:4G; SUGAR:4G

OTHER FAVORITE RECIPES

Tangy Chicken Sandwiches

Servings: 4
Cooking Time: 20 Minutes
Ingredients:

- 2 lbs. chicken breast, sliced into 4 cutlets
- 4 potato buns, toasted
- For the marinade:
- 1/2 cup pickle juice
- 1 tablespoon dijon mustard
- 1 teaspoon paprika
- 1/2 teaspoon black pepper
- 1/2 teaspoon salt

Directions:
1. Mix marinade ingredients together in a mixing bowl.
2. Place chicken in marinade and marinate for 30 minutes in the refrigerator.
3. Preheat griddle to medium-high. Wipe off extra marinade and sear chicken for 7 minutes per side, or until a meat thermometer reaches 165°F.
4. Allow chicken to rest for 5 minutes after grilling and serve on toasted buns.

Nutrition Info: Calories:265, Sodium:685 mg, Dietary Fiber: 0.6 g, Fat: 6g, Carbs:1.1g, Protein: 48.4g.

- 1 teaspoon cayenne pepper
- 1 teaspoon curry powder
- 1 teaspoon turmeric
- 1 teaspoon ground ginger
- 1 teaspoon ground cumin
- 1 tablespoon Mexene chili powder
- 1 tablespoon paprika
- dash of nutmeg
- LAST ROUNDUP BEEF RUB
- Caleb Pirtle III, Dallas, Texas
- ½ teaspoon lemon pepper
- ¼ teaspoon ground rosemary
- 4 teaspoons garlic powder
- 4 teaspoons onion powder
- 1 tablespoon Worcestershire powder *
- 1 teaspoon paprika
- 1 teaspoon beef bouillon granules
- 2 teaspoons Montreal Steak Seasoning
- 2 teaspoons salt
- 2 tablespoons black pepper, coarsely ground

Directions:
1. Preparing the Ingredients.
2. Combine all the ingredients in a large bowl, mixing well. Use immediately or store tightly sealed in glass, or plastic, container. Shake before each use to re-mix the spices.

Red River Rub

Servings: 8
Ingredients:

- Casablanca Rub
- 2 tablespoons paprika
- 1 teaspoon salt
- 1 teaspoon sugar
- ½ teaspoon coarsely ground black pepper
- ½ teaspoon ground ginger
- ½ teaspoon ground cardamom
- ½ teaspoon ground cumin
- ½ teaspoon ground fenugreek
- ½ teaspoon ground cloves
- ¼ teaspoon ground cinnamon
- ¼ teaspoon ground allspice
- ¼ teaspoon cayenne pepper
- RED RIVER RUB

Grilled Ratta-tooey

Servings: 4
Ingredients:

- 1 medium eggplant, about 1 pound
- 2 medium onions, Walla Wall, Vidalia or Maui preferred
- 1 medium summer squash or zucchini
- 1 large golden or red bell pepper
- 2 tablespoons olive oil
- 1 large ripe tomato, seeded and diced
- ¼ cup chopped black olives
- 2 tablespoons chopped fresh basil
- 2 tablespoons chopped fresh cilantro
- 1 teaspoon fines herbes
- 1 teaspoon oregano
- 2 tablespoons red wine vinegar

- sea or coarse salt to taste
- freshly ground pepper to taste
- ¼ pound asiago cheese

Directions:

1. Preparing the Ingredients.
2. Cut the eggplant into ½-inch-thick slices. Salt them on both sides and place them in a colander for 30 Minutes, then rinse and drain. You may cut off the peel if you wish.
3. Peel the onions and cut them in ½ inch slices. Quarter the summer squash or zucchini lengthwise. Cut the bell pepper into ½-inch pieces lengthwise.
4. Grilling
5. Prepare a hot grill (500° to 600°). Brush the vegetables lightly with the olive oil. Grill the eggplant on both sides until nicely browned and quite tender, about 12-15 Minutes total. Grill the onions, bell pepper, and zucchini on both sides until they're tender and marked with brown, about 10 Minutes total. Remove the veggies from the grill, place in a medium bowl and let cool. When all the vegetables are cool enough to handle, chop them into fairly large chunks and combine them in a serving bowl.
6. Mix in the tomato, olives, basil, cilantro, fines herbes, olive oil, and vinegar, and toss well. Season to taste with salt and pepper. If desired, sprinkle the top with crumbled asiago cheese. Serve at room temperature with grilled garlic bread or foccacia bread.

Flounder Spaghetti

Servings: 6
Cooking Time: 30 Minutes
Ingredients:

- 1 lb. spaghetti
- 1 lb. flounder fillet
- 4 cloves garlic, sliced 1/4 cup extra virgin olive oil
- 1/2 cup parsley, chopped
- 1/2 tsp. red pepper flakes

Directions:

1. Cook spaghetti according to the box directions.
2. Griddle grill the flounder on medium heat to desired doneness.
3. In a separate pot, sauté the garlic in olive oil until lightly golden.
4. Add cooked pasta, parsley, red pepper flakes, and flounder to the pot. Season with salt and pepper.
5. Serve spaghetti with lemon wedges.

Nutrition Info: (Per serving):Calories 270.2, Fat 10.7 g, carbs 8g, protein 18g

Beach Peanut Salad

Servings: 4
Ingredients:

- 1 small head of cabbage, finely chopped
- 2 cups finely chopped unsalted peanuts (or pecans or walnuts)
- 1 teaspoons butter
- 1 teaspoons mustard
- 1 teaspoons brown sugar
- 1 teaspoons whole wheat flour
- ¾ teaspoons pepper
- 4 tablespoons apple cider vinegar
- 2 egg yolks, Whisken salt

Directions:

1. Preparing the Ingredients
2. In a medium bowl mix the chopped cabbage and peanuts together and set aside.
3. Grilling
4. Cream the butter, mustard, sugar and flour together until a thick paste, then add the pepper and mix in the vinegar. In a double boiler heat this mixture while stirring, until very thick. Add Whisken egg yolks, salt to taste, and mix thoroughly. When mixed and while still warm, pour over nuts and cabbage, toss gently and serve.

Salmon Burgers

Servings: 4
Cooking Time: 15 Minutes
Ingredients:

- 4 potato buns
- 2 lbs salmon, finely chopped
- 1/2 red onion, finely chopped
- 1 stalk celery, finely chopped
- 1/2 teaspoon garlic powder
- 2 teaspoons dijon mustard

- 1 teaspoon salt
- 4 slices tomato
- 2 tablespoons vegetable oil

Directions:

1. In a large bowl, combine the chopped salmon, onion, celery, garlic powder, mustard, and salt. Mix well and form into 4 equal patties.

2. Heat your griddle to medium heat and add the vegetable oil. When oil is shimmering add the salmon patties, cooking 6 to 7 minutes per side. Remove from the griddle, place on the buns and top with sliced tomato to serve.

Nutrition Info: Calories: 512, Sodium: 935 mg, Dietary Fiber: 3.7g Fat: 22.5g, Carbs: 32.4g Protein: 49.5g

Orange Cornish Hen

Servings: 2

Cooking Time: 60 Minutes

Ingredients:

- 1 cornish hen
- 1/4 onion, cut into chunks
- 1/4 orange cut into wedges
- 2 garlic cloves
- 4 fresh sage leaves
- 1 1/2 fresh rosemary sprigs
- For glaze:
- 2-star anise
- 1 tbsp honey
- 1 cup orange juice
- 1/4 fresh orange, sliced
- 1/2 orange zest
- 1.5 oz Grand Marnier
- 1/2 cinnamon stick

Directions:

1. Stuff hen with orange wedges, garlic, onions, and herbs. Season with pepper and salt.

2. Preheat the griddle to high heat.

3. Spray griddle top with cooking spray.

4. Place hen on hot griddle top and cook for 60 minutes or until the internal temperature of hens reaches 165 F.

5. Meanwhile, in a saucepan heat, all glaze ingredients until reduce by half over medium-high heat.

6. Brush hen with glaze.

7. Slice and serve.

Nutrition Info: (Per Serving): Calories 351 ;Fat 12.1 g ;Carbohydrates 29.2 g ;Sugar 40.9 g ;Protein 16 g ;Cholesterol 85 mg

Seafood Rub

Servings: 2

Ingredients:

- ⅓ cup (88 g) coarse flake salt
- ⅓ cup (36 g) paprika
- ¼ cup (39 g) garlic powder
- ¼ cup (28 g) freshly ground pepper
- 2 tbsp (5 g) dried thyme
- 2 tbsp (7 g) dried rosemary
- 2 tbsp (16 g) ground chipotle pepper
- 2 tbsp (14 g) onion powder

Directions:

1. Preparing the Ingredients.

2. Fresh seafood is the best, and with this rub we try to showcase the depth of flavor in our dish and not overpower it. We want every bite to have the same flavor and depth to which you are accustomed. This rub is fabulous on shrimp and salmon. We also use it when we make a low-country boil. Add the salt, paprika, garlic, pepper, thyme, rosemary, chipotle pepper and onion to a small bowl; mix well. Store in an airtight container for up to 6 months.

Savory Chicken Burgers

Servings: 3

Cooking Time: 20 Minutes

Ingredients:

- 1 lb. ground chicken
- 1/2 red onion, finely chopped
- 1 teaspoon garlic powder
- 1/2 teaspoon onion powder
- 1/4 teaspoon black pepper
- 1/2 teaspoon salt
- 3 tablespoons vegetable oil
- 3 potato buns, toasted

Directions:

1. In a large bowl, combine the ground chicken, onion, garlic powder, onion powder, pepper, and salt.

Mix well to combine. Form the chicken mixture into three equal patties. Don't work the mixture too much or the burgers will be too dense.

2.   Heat your griddle to medium-high heat. Add the vegetable oil.

3.   When the oil is shimmering, add the chicken patties and cook 5 minutes per side, or until the patties reach 165°F.

4.   Remove the patties from the griddle and allow to rest for five minutes before serving on the toasted buns.

Nutrition Info: Calories: 420, Sodium: 519 mg, Dietary Fiber: 0.6 g, Fat: 24.8g, Carbs: 2.8g, Protein: 44.2g.

Bbq White Sauce

Servings: 16
Cooking Time: 10 Minutes
Ingredients:

- Mayonnaise – 1-1/2 cups.
- Horseradish – 2 tsps.
- Worcestershire sauce – 1 tsp.
- Brown sugar – 1 tbsp.
- Spicy brown mustard – 1 tbsp.
- Onion powder –1/2 tsp.
- Garlic powder –1/2 tsp.
- Apple cider vinegar – 1/4 cup.
- Salt – 1 tsp.

Directions:

1.   Add all ingredients into a mixing bowl and whisk until smooth. Pour sauce into an air-tight container and store in the refrigerator for up to 1 week.

Nutrition Info: (Per serving):Calories 156, Carbs 1g, Fat 17g, Protein 1g

Caesar Salad Poultry Burgers

Servings: 4
Cooking Time: 15 Minutes
Ingredients:

- ¼ cup mayonnaise
- 2 cloves garlic, 1 minced, 1 peeled and left
- whole
- 2 oil-packed anchovy fillets, drained and mashed
- 2 tablespoons freshly grated Parmesan cheese
- 1 tablespoon fresh lemon juice
- ½ teaspoon Worcestershire sauce
- 1½ pounds ground chicken or turkey
- Good-quality vegetable oil for oiling the grates
- 4 ciabatta rolls, split, or 8–10 slider buns
- Good-quality olive oil for brushing the rolls
- 1 leaves heart of romaine, trimmed

Directions:

1.   Preparing the Ingredients.

2.   1 Line a baking sheet with wax paper. Whisk the mayonnaise, minced garlic, anchovies, Parmesan, lemon juice, and Worcestershire together in a small bowl until smooth. Put the chicken in a medium bowl and add 2 tablespoons of the dressing. Cover and refrigerate the remaining dressing. Work the dressing into the chicken with your hands gently but completely. Form the mixture into 4 burgers ¾ to 1 inch thick. Put them on the prepared pan, cover, and refrigerate until firm, at least 1 hour.

3.   Turn control knob to the high position, when the griddle is hot, brush the cut sides of the rolls with olive oil. Brush the burgers with oil on both sides, put them on the griddle. Carefully turning once with two spatulas, until browned on the outside and no longer pink in the center, 5 to 7 Minutes per side.

4.   2 For the last couple of Minutes, toast the rolls on the grill, cut side down. To serve, rub the cut side of the top of each roll with the whole garlic clove. Put a burger on the bottom half, add a dollop of the remaining dressing, a leaf of romaine, and the top of the roll.

New Mexican Salsa Verde

Servings: 1 Cup
Cooking Time: 15 Minutes
Ingredients:

- 4 cloves garlic (leave the skins on),
- skewered on a wooden toothpick or small bamboo skewer
- 1 cup roasted New Mexican green chiles or Anaheim chiles cut into ¼-inch strips (8 to 10 chiles
- 2 tablespoons chopped fresh cilantro
- 2 teaspoons fresh lime juice, or more to
- taste
- ½ teaspoon ground cumin

- ½ teaspoon dried oregano
- Coarse salt (kosher or sea) and freshly
- ground black pepper

Directions:

1. Preparing the Ingredients.
2. Preheat the griddle to high. When ready to cook, lightly oil the grill surface. Place the burgers on the hot griddle. The burgers will be done after cooking 4 to 6 Minutes. Put the garlic cloves until they are lightly browned and tender, 2 to 3 Minutes per side (4 to 6 Minutes in all). Scrape any really burnt skin off the garlic. Place the garlic, chile strips, cilantro, lime juice, cumin, oregano, and 4 tablespoons of water in a blender and purée until smooth, scraping down the sides of the blender with a spatula.
3. Transfer the salsa to a saucepan and bring to a gentle simmer over medium heat. Let simmer until thick and flavorful, 5 to 8 Minutes, stirring with a wooden spoon. The salsa should be thick (roughly the consistency of heavy cream) but pourable; add more water as needed. Taste for seasoning, adding more lime juice as necessary and salt and pepper to taste; the salsa should be highly seasoned.

Rosemary Butter Cornish Hens

Servings: 2
Cooking Time: 60 Minutes
Ingredients:

- 1 cornish hen, rinse and pat dry with paper towels
- 1 tbsp butter, melted
- 1 rosemary sprigs
- 1 tsp poultry seasoning

Directions:

1. Stuff rosemary sprigs into the hen cavity.
2. Brush hen with melted butter and season with poultry seasoning.
3. Preheat the griddle to high heat.
4. Spray griddle top with cooking spray.
5. Place hen on hot griddle top and cook for 60 minutes or until the internal temperature of hens reaches 165 F.
6. Slice and serve.

Nutrition Info: (Per Serving): Calories 127 ;Fat 8 g ;Carbohydrates 0.5 g ;Sugar 0 g ;Protein 13 g ;Cholesterol 74 mg

Pork Tenderloin Sandwiches

Servings: 6
Cooking Time: 25 Minutes
Ingredients:

- 2 (3/4-lb.) pork tenderloins
- 1 teaspoon garlic powder
- 1 teaspoon sea salt
- 1 teaspoon dry mustard
- 1/2 teaspoon coarsely ground pepper
- Olive oil, for brushing
- 6 whole wheat hamburger buns
- 6 tablespoons barbecue sauce

Directions:

1. Stir the garlic, salt, pepper, and mustard together in a small mixing bowl.
2. Rub pork tenderloins evenly with olive oil, then seasoning mix.
3. Preheat griddle to medium-high heat, and cook 10 to 12 minutes on each side or until a meat thermometer inserted into thickest portion registers 155°F.
4. Remove from grill and let stand 10 minutes.
5. Slice thinly, and evenly distribute onto hamburger buns.
6. Drizzle each sandwich with barbecue sauce and serve.

Nutrition Info: Calories: 372, Sodium: 694 mg, Dietary Fiber: 2.9g, Fat: 13.4g, Carbs: 24.7g Protein: 37.2g

Big Burger

Servings: 4
Cooking Time: 9 Minutes
Ingredients:

- 1¼ pounds lean ground beef
- ½ teaspoon salt
- ½ teaspoon freshly ground black pepper
- Seasoning of your choice (such as a dash of Worcestershire or hot sauce, or 1 teaspoon Spicy Spanish Rub

- 4 slices cheese such as American, cheddar, or Swiss (about 4 ounces), or ¼ cup
- crumbled blue or goat cheese
- 4 toasted buns
- 4 beefsteak tomato slices
- 4 leaves romaine lettuce

Directions:

1. Preparing the Ingredients.
2. Bring the griddle grill to medium-high heat.
3. Put the beef in a medium bowl and add the salt, pepper, and your preferred seasonings. Using a fork, mix the seasonings into the meat and then, with your hands, form the mixture into 4 patties, each about 1 inch thick.
4. When the grill is hot, place the burgers on the Grill and cook for 4 Minutes without flipping. Cooking is complete when the internal temperature of the beef reaches at least 145°F on a food thermometer. If needed, cook for up to 5 more Minutes.
5. Lay the cheese over the burgers and lower the grill. Grill for 30 seconds, just until the cheese melts.
6. Set the burgers onto the bottom halves of the buns, add a slice of tomato and a leaf of lettuce to each burger, and cover with the tops of the buns. Serve immediately.

Nutrition Info: (Per Serving): CALORIES: 510; FAT: 30G; PROTEIN: 36G

Citrus Based Suce (ponzu)

Servings: 1½

Ingredients:

- ½ cup soy sauce
- ¼ cup fresh lemon juice
- ¼ cup fresh lime juice
- ¼ cup dried bonito flakes, or one 4-inch piece kombu
- 2 tablespoons mirin (or 1 tablespoon each honey and water mixed together)
- 2 tablespoons rice vinegar

Directions:

1. Preparing the Ingredients.
2. Beat all the ingredients together in a small bowl. Cover and refrigerate overnight.

3. Strain into an airtight container and refrigerate until you're ready to use it, for up to several days.

Carolina Q Sauce

Servings: 5

Ingredients:

- 4 cups apple cider vinegar
- ¼ cup honey
- ¼ cup yellow mustard
- 4 tablespoons brown sugar
- 4 teaspoons sea salt
- 4 teaspoons crushed red pepper flakes
- 2 teaspoon coarse black pepper

Directions:

1. Preparing the Ingredients.
2. In a large saucepan-
3. Grilling
4. over low heat, add all the ingredients and simmer all for 15-20 Minutes, stirring constantly with a spoon. DON'T BOIL!
5. Remove pan from the heat, and let pan cool to room temperature. Pour mixture into a sealable glass or plastic bottle.
6. Fantastic with smoked ham, pork shoulder, or pork ribs. But should be tried on beef, lamb and chicken too.

Rosemary Mustard Marinade

Servings: 1

Ingredients:

- 6 sprigs fresh rosemary
- 1 cup tarragon vinegar
- 6 tablespoon Dijon mustard
- 2 tablespoon minced garlic
- pepper to taste
- salt to taste
- 2 tablespoons olive oil

Directions:

1. Preparing the Ingredients.
2. Beat all ingredients together in a medium bowl. Use this as a marinade for beef, chicken, lamb, pork (shoulder is wonderful in this marinade), or firm fish steaks Marinate at least 6 hours or, preferably, overnight.

Cheese-stuffed

Servings: 6

Ingredients:

- ¼ cup bleu cheese
- 10 slices bacon

Directions:

1. Preparing the Ingredients.
2. ¼ cup bleu cheese 1. Preheat the oven to 400° F. ¼ cup cream cheese Mix the cheeses together. Set aside.20 dates 3. Make a slit, lengthwise, into each date. Stuff with cheese mixture. 10 slices bacon, raw, cut in half 4. Roll each date with bacon. Grill 2-3 Minutes on each side.
3. Grilling
4. Cook in the oven for 8-10 Minutes or until bacon is crispy. I'll add a shelled pistachio or walnut into each date for an extra crunch.

Nut Burgers

Servings: 4

Cooking Time: 10 Minutes

Ingredients:

- 1 cup raw rolled oats or cooked short-grain white or brown rice
- 1 cup walnuts, pecans, almonds, cashews, or other nuts
- 1 medium onion, cut into pieces
- 1 teaspoon chili powder
- 1 egg
- 2 tablespoons ketchup, miso, tomato
- paste, nut butter, or tahini
- Salt and pepper
- Broth, soy sauce, wine, or other liquid if
- necessary

Directions:

1. Preparing the Ingredients.
2. 1 Put the onion in a food processor and pulse to a paste. Add the nuts and oats and pulse to chop, but not too finely. Add the ketchup, chili powder, some salt and pepper, and the egg. Process briefly; don't grind the mixture too finely.
3. Add a little liquid—water, broth, soy sauce, wine, whatever is handy—if necessary; the mixture should

be moist enough to hold together without being wet. With damp hands, shape the mixture into 8 burgers; put on a platter without touching and refrigerate for at least 1 hour.

4. 2 Turn control knob to the high position, when the griddle is hot, put them and cook, carefully turning once with two spatulas, until browned on the outside and no longer pink in the center, 5 to 7 Minutes per side.

Rosemary Hen

Servings: 2

Cooking Time: 60 Minutes

Ingredients:

- 1 cornish game hen
- 1 tbsp butter, melted
- 1/2 tbsp rosemary, minced
- 1 tsp chicken rub

Directions:

1. Brush hens with melted butter.
2. Mix together rosemary and chicken rub.
3. Rub hen with rosemary and chicken rub mixture.
4. Preheat the griddle to high heat.
5. Spray griddle top with cooking spray.
6. Place hen on hot griddle top and cook for 60 minutes or until internal temperature reaches 165 F.
7. Serve and enjoy.

Nutrition Info: (Per Serving): Calories 221 ;Fat 17 g ;Carbohydrates 0.5 g ;Sugar 0 g ;Protein 14.5 g ;Cholesterol 100 mg

Traditional Bbq Sauce

Servings: 3

Ingredients:

- 2 cups (480 ml) tomato ketchup
- ¼ cup (60 ml) apple cider vinegar
- ¼ cup (55 g) brown sugar
- 2 tbsp (30 g) yellow mustard
- ¼ cup (60 ml) honey

Directions:

1. Preparing the Ingredients.
2. This is a great sauce recipe to use on beef, ribs and poultry. It is also a starting point for dreaming up your own sauce and flavor profiles. Get creative and

feel free to try various combinations. If you like to bring the heat, introduce cayenne or chili powder to the recipe.

3.   Combine the ketchup, vinegar, sugar, mustard and honey in a small bowl; mix well. Refrigerate the sauce until ready to use. Any unused sauce can be stored in a jar or airtight container in the refrigerator for 2 weeks.

Marvelous Margarita Glaze

Servings: 1

Ingredients:

- ½ cup triple sec
- ½ cup lime juice
- ½ cup tequila
- ½ cup honey
- pinch of salt

Directions:

1.   Preparing the Ingredients.
2.   Mix all ingredients in a medium saucepan over low heat.
3.   Grilling
4.   Stirring constantly, for 4 to 5 Minutes. When the glaze is thoroughly mixed, remove from the heat and cool. When cooled you can bottle or use the glaze straight from the pan to brush over chicken, fish, or shellfish.
5.   Try basting shrimp with this, or use this as a dip for cooked chicken wings or shrimp. One more way to use is to spryd the glaze on grilled oysters or clams, after the shells have opened.

Flank Steak With Balsamic Onion Dressing

Servings: 4

Cooking Time: 20 Minutes

Ingredients:

- 1 Flank Steak
- 1 Tsp. Sea Salt
- 1 Tsp. Ground Black Pepper
- 2 Tbsp. Olive Oil
- Balsamic Onion Dressing

Directions:

1.   Rub flank steak with sea salt, pepper, and olive oil.

2.   Mix dressing ingredients together.
3.   Remove onions from dressing and grill until tender. Cut onions into quarters before returning to the dressing.
4.   Griddle grill the steaks to desired temperature.
5.   Let steaks rest before slicing. Drizzle with dressing before serving with your favorite side dish.
Nutrition Info: (Per serving):Calories278.8, Protein 96g Carbs 30g Fat 28g

Tybet's Sauce

Servings: 1

Ingredients:

- 1 can cola (12 oz.) DO NOT USE DIET SODAS
- 1½ cups ketchup
- 1 cup finely chopped onion
- ¼ cup cider vinegar
- ⅛ cup A1 steak sauce
- 1 teaspoon Mexene chili powder
- 2 teaspoon lemon granules
- 1 teaspoon white sugar
- 1 teaspoon salt
- white pepper to taste

Directions:

1.   Preparing the Ingredients.
2.   In a medium saucepan, over high heat, combine all the ingredients and bring to a boil, stirring often.
3.   Grilling
4.   Immediately reduce the heat to low and simmer, covered, stirring occasionally, for 30-45 Minutes or until sauce is thickened. Remove pan from heat, let mixture cool, and then store in a tightly covered glass jar or plastic container.

Vital Bar-be-cue Sauce

Servings: 5

Ingredients:

- 1 lg. finely chopped Vidalia onion (or Maui, or Walla Walla)
- 1 cup apple cider vinegar
- ½ cup apple cider
- ¼ cup lemon juice
- ⅓ cup distilled (white) vinegar
- 5 tablespoons prepared yellow mustard

- 3 teaspoons A-1 sauce
- 4 tablespoons honey
- 2 teaspoons brown sugar
- 3 cups ketchup
- 1 teaspoon mesquite seasoning salt *
- 1 teaspoon black pepper
- ¼ pound butter, or margarine

Directions:
1. Preparing the Ingredients.
2. In a medium saucepan mix all ingredients together well, and.
3. Grilling
4. simmer for 10-15 Minutes, stirring often. This sauce works especially well with beef but can be used for just about any Griddle meat, poultry, or fish.

Superior Rosemary Polenta

Servings: 4

Ingredients:
- 24-oz. log prepared polenta
- 2 teaspoon extra-virgin olive oil
- garlic salt to taste
- lemon pepper to taste
- 2 tablespoons chopped rosemary

Directions:
1. Preparing the Ingredients.
2. Preheat Griddle on high.
3. Cut the polenta into 12½-inch thick slices. Place the slices on a baking sheet. Brush both sides of the polenta rounds with oil and season lightly with garlic salt, lemon pepper, and sprinkle with chopped rosemary leaves. Lightly oil the grill rack and.
4. Grilling
5. Polenta slices over high heat (500° to 600°) until nicely browned, 3 to 5 Minutes per side.
6. Remove from heat and serve on a heated platter.

Grilled Tomato Vinaigrette

Servings: 4

Ingredients:
- 12 slices bacon 2 pears, cored & cut in half
- Tomato Vinaigrette 6 plum tomatoes
- cut in half ½ cup extra virgin olive oil 1 tsp
- sea salt ½ tsp
- ground black pepper 3 cloves garlic
- peeled & sliced 3 tbsp. red wine vinegar

Directions:
1. Preparing the Ingredients.
2. Grill bacon until crispy. Set aside.
3. Grilling
4. Grill pears in remaining bacon fat. Vinaigrette: in a bowl, combine tomatoes, olive oil, sea salt, pepper, and garlic. Reserve vinegar for later. Remove tomatoes and garlic from vinaigrette. Grill to desired doneness. Return garlic to vinaigrette. Once cool, chop tomatoes and return to the vinaigrette. Add vinegar and mix gently. In a separate bowl, toss arugula with vinaigrette, bleu cheese, and pumpkins seeds. Divide salad onto 4 plates. Top each with three slices bacon and half a pear before serving. 6 cups baby arugula ½ cup crumbled bleu cheese, 1/3 cup pumpkin seeds, toasted.

APPENDIX : RECIPES INDEX

Spare Ribs With Sweet Ancho-cumin Rub 64
Spicy Egg Scrambled 13
Spicy Grilled Squid 67
Spicy Lemon Butter Shrimp 71
Spicy Soy Flank Steak 54
Spinach Pancakes 9
Steak & Mushrooms 56
Steak 31
Steak With Green Chimichurri 56
Stir Fry Bok Choy 92
Stir Fry Cabbage 103
Stir Fry Vegetables 93
Straw Berries Pizza 80
Strawberries Romanoff 87
Strawberry Shortcake 87
Strawberry, Banana, Crepes 19
Stuffed Cabbage With Summer Vegetables 93
Stuffed French Toast 89
Stuffed Winter Squash With Quinoa, Green
Beans, And Tomatoes 95
Succulent Griddle-seared Garlic Tenderloin 58
Sugared Peaches With Candied Ginger Ice
Cream 83
Summer Shrimp Salad 76
Summer Squash With Sea Salt 29
Superior Rosemary Polenta 113
Sweet Potato Pancakes 85
Sweet Thai Cilantro Chili Chicken Quarters 42
Swordfish 72

T

Tangy Chicken Sandwiches 105

Tarragon Chicken Tenders 39
Tasty Chicken Patties 46
Tasty Herb Mushrooms 79
Tasty Shrimp Skewers 70
Tender Steak With Pineapple Rice 54
Teriyaki Chicken And Veggie Rice Bowls 48
Thai-style Coleslaw 23
Thick Stacked Sizzling Burgers On The Griddle
56
Tomato Melts With Spinach Salad 91
Tomato Scrambled Egg 17
Tomatoes With Basil 32
Traditional Bbq Sauce 111
Tuna With Fresh Tomato-basil Sauce 67
Tybet's Sauce 112

U

Ultimate Breakfast Burrito 8
Upside-down Plum Cake 17

V

Vital Bar-be-cue Sauce 112

W

Watermelon Steaks With Rosemary 100
Watermelon With Honey And Lime 88
Whole Fish With Basil-orange Oil 68
Whoopie Pies 86

Y

Yucatan-style Grilled Pork 64
Yummy Turkey Burger 81

Z

Zucchini Antipasto 91